MASTERY
OF
AWARENESS

MASTERY
OF
AWARENESS

Living the Agreements

Doña Bernadette Vigil

with Arlene Broska, Ph.D.

Illustrations by doña Bernadette Vigil

Foreword by don Miguel Ruiz, author of
The Four Agreements

Bear & Company
Rochester, Vermont

Bear & Company
One Park Street
Rochester, Vermont 05767
www.InnerTraditions.com

*Note to the reader: This book is intended as an informational guide. The approaches
and techniques described herein are not meant to be a substitute for professional
medical care or psychiatric treatment.*

Library of Congress Cataloging-in-Publication Data

Vigil, Bernadette

  The mastery of awareness : living the agreements / Bernadette Vigil
with Arlene Broska; foreword by Miguel Ruiz.

    p   c.m.

  ISBN 1-879181-61-4 (paper)

  1. Conduct of life. 2. Toltec philosophy—Miscellanea. I. Broska, Arlene.
  II. Title.

  BJ1581.2.V47 2001

  299'.792—dc21

                                                          2001016210

Printed and bound in the United States

10 9 8 7 6 5 4 3 2 1

Text design and layout by Rachel Goldenberg
This book was typeset in Deepdene with OptiEve as the display typeface
Cover painting: *The Direction of the West*, by Bernadette Vigil

THE GRANDMOTHERS

The
Grandmothers
of
Wisdom
Whispered in
my
ear
as the
Sound
of
their voices
echoed
in my heart
the echo
Cracked
a Doorway
to a place
that only
the
Grandmothers
can share

the birth

hole

of darkness & coldness,

as I am floating

in the veins

of the

Mother's Body

to

Become

every part of

her existence

to pass only

to know the

Secret,

Is only a

Joke

as The

Grandmothers

Laugh.

Doña Bernadette Vigil

CONTENTS

	FOREWORD BY DON MIGUEL RUIZ	ix
	ACKNOWLEDGMENTS	xiii
	INTRODUCTION	1
1	OVERVIEW	7
2	THE DOMESTICATION OF YOUR SOUL	15
3	THE JUDGE AND THE VICTIM	29
4	HOOKS AND MASKS	35
5	AGREEMENTS	45
6	EDUARDO	57
7	MIRRORS AND THE EXCHANGE OF ENERGY	63
8	MARY	73
9	THE STAR OF FREEDOM	83
10	THE ELEVEN AGREEMENTS OF THE SPIRITUAL WARRIOR	91
11	STALKING	113
12	THE SPIRAL	155

FOREWORD

The Mastery of Awareness is an excellent recapitulation of more than ten years of hard work on doña Bernadette's journey down the path of freedom. This is a fascinating description of the transformation of a woman who lived her life victimized by her own beliefs and judgments about the role of a woman in society.

Doña Bernadette began a rebellion against the suffering that women have endured for many centuries, a rebellion against the roles that many women have assumed as helpless victims of society. In her lifetime, she saw many women who had become victims condemned to suffer endless abuse. Doña Bernadette did not want to become another victim of injustice, so she chose to seek the path of enlightenment and the path of the Spiritual Warrior.

On her journey, as doña Bernadette discovered the deception of her point of view and the self-abuse that it produced, she began to see the pain that all of her beliefs caused her. She had hidden for too long behind the masks of righteousness, pride, and vanity. Recovering her awareness was an extremely painful acknowledgment of the truth and the lies of her creation. In this book, doña Bernadette describes every step of her long and dedicated journey with words spoken directly from the heart. With touching authenticity, she shares her transformation from a helpless victim into a woman of power and wisdom.

Doña Bernadette and I have worked together for more than ten years. In the early years she was part of a special group of four women who practiced the Mastery of Transformation or Stalking, which is part of the Mastery of Awareness. Doña Bernadette was my best apprentice and soon became a master and *nagual* woman of my party. The moment of her enlightenment occurred in Hawaii, and it was then that she chose to transform her point of view completely into one of love.

Since 1994 doña Bernadette has been guiding many apprentices to their freedom. For many years she was my main assistant in different power journeys, and now she is the leader of her own power journeys. The wisdom and love she has shared as a teacher in workshops and classes is now available in this book. Like the many people whose lives have been enriched by doña Bernadette's teachings, you may find in this book the opportunity to change the direction of your life.

Don Miguel Ruiz

ACKNOWLEDGMENTS

Gratitude and Respect
to the Mirrors Called Teachers

My mother, Aurora Leyva Vigil (saint); my father, Ramon Jose Duran Vigil (provider and rock); grandmothers Dolores Nieto Leyva (curandera and survivalist) and Dolores Duran Vigil (partera, midwife); Sister Julita; Dr. Sherrie Abend-Fels; Lama Karma Dorji; don Miguel Ruiz; doña Gaya Jenkins; Gurumayi; Sathya Sai Baba; the sunsets that transformed my vision of Awakening; the moon, stars, trees, and all the animals that shared their lives with me as tremendous Unconditional Love; and especially Hiquitie, and myself.

Fellow Mirrors

Doña Gaya Jenkins, North; myself, South; doña Gini Gentry, East; doña Rita Rivera, West.

Don Luis Molinar, Victoria Molinar, Trey Jenkins (Ramakrishna Ananda), don Pedro.

Acknowledgments

Comadres

Elena Avila, Gina Herrera, Reyna Luna, and Gabriela Lopez Waterman.

To the Warriors Who Trusted My Mirror

Arlene Broska, doña Wanda Lobito, don Nicola Prassinos, doña Margarita Sanchez, don Chris Dixon, don Alvaro Sanchez, Catharine Marzalik, Preetie Keel, Rhonan Heitzmann, David Norget, Tess Carvajal, Lennie Tan, Gayle Dawn Price, Liz Forrest, Gloria Valencia, Brandt Morgan, Mitra Sarhosh, Andrea Usher, M. Luisa Guerrero, Lynda Foishe, Michael Humphery, Rudy Miera, Sandra Grueiro, Heidi Shepherd, Christinea Johnson, Jean Rael, Kate Dow Gaur, Manish Gaur, Mersedeh Kheradmand, Federique Botermans, Gabby Peprisan, Samuel Rutenberg, Luis Kahn, Sandra Lee Tatum, Viola Vigil, Belinda Trujillo, Jeanne and Jennifer Jenkins, Tita Weems, Brian Claro, Juan Antonio Lopez, Wilma Leon, Tomas Reale, Patricia Klesinger, Dolores Vigil Cruz, Alicia Maes, Pat Lessard, Deidre Bainbridge, and Gerard.

Special Thanks

Inner Traditions International and Bear & Company; Arlene Broska; and Barbara Moulton.

Introduction

My desire to become a Spiritual Warrior on the Toltec path began during my search for happiness and contentment when I was young. In my early years, I was always searching for something. I took a lot of risks and often felt like I was going against society's belief systems. There was always some kind of struggle inside of me. I didn't feel happy or content in life. When I was very young, I believed strongly in the Catholic Church and followed its teaching with all my heart. I explored becoming a cloistered nun or monk. I also visited other churches to see what their intentions were, what their words were, and what their love was. None of them spoke to me.

Finally, I had an awakening when my partner came and told me that our relationship was over. My heart was broken. Out of sadness and self-pity, I decided to go inner tubing up in the mountains. My first time down the mountain on the inner tube, I broke six ribs and was hospitalized. It was New Year's Eve. There was a full moon, and it was a blue moon. That was in 1990. My ex-partner would not come to see me in the hospital, and I had only a few visitors. My life felt very empty. I realized that I was really truly alone, and that all of us as human beings must go through our individual processes alone, even when other people are around us.

As a child I had seen visions and spirits. In 1990, as I lay in the hospital bed, I saw images of Jesus on the cross, falling at the speed of light. The visions helped me look at my life. Even though I felt heartbroken that my partner didn't want to be with me, I realized there was something more to life. My life was not about trying to make somebody happy, or wanting somebody to make me happy. I realized that I had to find happiness inside myself. This became my intent. I wanted to feel total contentment and peace, so much so that it wouldn't matter if a partner stayed or left. If a partner chose to leave, it wouldn't ever again take my happiness away. Nothing would.

My accident was an awakening from Spirit, and not really an accident. Spirit was always talking to me, but I just didn't listen, as most people don't. I needed to experience a shake-up in my physical body so that I would have no place to run. I was forced to sit still for weeks in order to heal. That sitting became a time of contemplation and looking at myself. As soon as my six broken ribs healed, I went to the K.S.K. Tibetan Buddhist Center and studied with Lama Karma Dorje for a while. I learned how to meditate. Several months later a friend told me about Don Miguel, a shaman who had come into town. I went to a lecture and then began to study with him. The work was powerful for me. I put 100 percent into it; I had nothing lose.

While studying with Don Miguel, I took my first power journey to the pyramids of Teotihuacan. I participated in a ceremony of Toltec warriors in the place where they had held ceremonies thousands of years ago. My life began to transform every moment. After the trip, Don Miguel asked me if I wanted to become an apprentice. There were very few apprentices at that time. I agreed. Don Miguel chose four of the women who were studying with him to represent the four directions; I was the South. We began weekly Stalking groups at my home, a beautiful little adobe house that had no electricity and used a woodstove for heat. Many months later another woman and a man who was being trained as a *nagual* joined us. We met no matter what: snow, rain, or shine. We gave our words to look at ourselves, and we practiced Stalking for almost two years. We shared our lives. We healed together, and we loved and respected each other as mirrors. We also learned a new level of love and respect for ourselves. Our work took great discipline and a true desire to look within. It required a lot of focus and surrendering.

By my third year of apprenticeship, I had done a lot of Stalking. I had claimed more and more personal power and had gone on a lot of power journeys with Don Miguel and Doña Gaya, the nagual woman at that time. Doña Gaya was a very powerful, loving person who was very direct, a magical teacher. The most life-changing power journey I took with Don Miguel and Doña Gaya was to Hawaii. We walked with a group of Spiritual Warriors for three hours down into a volcano, where Don Miguel did a ceremony. During the ceremony something happened to Don Miguel. I found out later that he was having a major heart attack. All I knew at the time was that he was not in his usual form of power, and that Doña Gaya had already left to begin the walk out of the volcano.

My instincts and inner wisdom told me there was something I had to do because I felt that Don Miguel was leaving his body. I had no telephone or contact with anyone but the Spiritual Warriors who were there, and we had to walk for three hours to get out of the volcano. Also, the majority of my companions were beginning Spiritual Warriors, so I could not tell them anything and I had to keep them focused. At that moment I chose to help Don Miguel by pulling the energy from Mother Earth into my womb and placing my hands on him. I was able to pull in a lot of energy because Hawaii is such a tremendous source of pure Mother Earth energy. By sharing my love and energy with Don Miguel, our spirits merged and we became one being. We then began a slow walk out of the volcano. I felt like I was walking with Jesus toward his crucifixion, the moment of transformation when he would leave his physical body. At that time Don Miguel almost did leave his physical body. As we walked I also saw Don Miguel shift and become different beings from different lives. Additionally, I saw and felt the guardians from the rocks sending energy to my Will. We finally made it out of the volcano and to the van.

With that experience my whole being transformed and shifted. No words could truly describe it, but I felt a great happiness from giving of myself for another human being's survival. It was the most unconditional expression of love. From the moment when my and Don Miguel's spirits merged, I became the second nagual woman (Doña Gaya was the first). It had never been my dream to become a realized nagual woman. I had not known that I was born a nagual, a being with a double egg, or energy field. It was simply my dream to become joyous and peaceful with every breath. I wanted no situation to ever take away my happiness because my happiness would be within me. In the giving of my love and energy for Don Miguel's survival, I received the greatest gift. I experienced true joy and unconditional love. From that moment on, I became a teacher. Since that time, I have shared with and served many, many Spiritual Warriors who are now grand teachers themselves. I am now peaceful in my life with every breath. Nothing can take away my happiness, because it is within me.

With this book I share with you the journey to realize your true nature. Your true nature is happiness, and your true spirit is joyful and self-loving. Once you truly love yourself, you can love others unconditionally with no expectations. This book guides you to look into your heart and to open those doors that you have locked. To be content, you must have the courage to unlock those doors and to love the parts of you that are behind them. I give you this book with all my love and respect.

1

OVERVIEW

The Dream of the Planet

THE TOLTECS BELIEVED THAT WE LIVE LIFE IN A DREAM. They saw that most people live in the Dream of the Planet, or the belief systems of everyday life. The Toltecs also believed that we could become masterful warriors and transcend the Dream of the Planet with its limitations to create our own limitless Dream. For us, the Dream of the Planet is our world as we know it today. It is our societies, our governments, our belief systems, and our rules and expectations. It is the structures by which we live our lives, set our goals, and strive to obtain certain things in life, such as good jobs, families, nice homes, education, status, and so on. Within this Dream may be certain basic beliefs, such as the one telling us that if we lead "good lives" and go to church/temple/mosque we will join God after death.

Although many societies today are materially rich, and we as individuals have so much in life, we are often still empty inside, searching for something more to make us happy. It is the rare one of us who feels content in life and yearns for nothing. This search for "something more" has led us to look toward spirituality, to find God, Spirit, the Source, or Jesus. We tend to believe that if we can connect with Spirit or God, we will find happiness, peace, contentment, or unconditional love, and therefore will no longer feel like something is missing.

Today, the greater openness to information outside traditional belief systems, or the Dream of the Planet, has resulted in the blossoming of many alternative beliefs. Spirituality is now in vogue. Now that we are in a new millennium, it is not a moment too soon. Our world as we know it is shifting; the energy is moving faster today than ever before on the planet. This period can be a time of tremendous transformation if we wake up to our true selves; or, it can be a time of tremendous devastation, tragedy, and discontentment if we are unwilling to face ourselves. There are many paths in existence, but the path that works for us is the one that opens the heart. We know it is the path for us when it makes us say, "Yes, that's my life." Then we feel a sense of peace, and the doors to the heart melt open. This book is written for each of us, so that we may say, "Yes, that's my life."

The Toltecs

The Toltecs were people of knowledge and wisdom; they were also artists of life. Their intent was to be masterful in every moment. Because of their tremendous love and respect for themselves, they created an impeccable environment—an environment of contentment. Looking inside themselves to heal the wounded Spiritual Warrior, they mastered a level of being fully alive and of creating heaven on earth. In every moment they were prepared to see the trees, the animals, and all of life inside and out, including beyond to the next level of God. The Toltecs felt that humans had the capacity to become masters, to believe in life without limitations, and to trust that there was something beyond what they already knew. These artists of life went on to create and be open to infinite love—the vision of all beings for peace of heart, mind, and breath.

There were two levels of Toltec apprenticeship: the Jaguar Knight and the Eagle Knight. Apprentices were guided by a *nagual*, a teacher of no limitations. The two levels represented stages at which the apprentices became their highest, true selves, and then reached beyond that point to experience never-ending unconditional love and contentment. Their first step on the journey was to choose to become apprentices at which time they became Jaguar Knights. To eventually reach the final level and experience unconditional love, the warriors had to master Stalking, Dreaming, and intent at each level of the work. This work of the Toltec warrior was called the Mastery of Awareness.

Many of the Toltec warriors were killed when the first conquerors arrived in Mexico. As a result, the practices of the Toltec path went underground, secret groups of Toltec warriors were created. Their teachings remained secret until very recently. Even in 1990, not just anybody could study the Toltec work. Only people who were chosen could become apprentices.

Stalking

But now it is time on earth for the wisdom of the Toltecs to be shared with everyone in the Dream of the Planet who is ready. You are one of these people if you are willing to be truthful with yourself, and to be who you really are. Freedom and love begin within you.

In this book you will take a dive into the Mastery of Awareness through practicing the art of Stalking. You can also choose to combine this art with other tools to find the God and love that you are. Stalking is a simple yet very powerful tool that can help you expand your awareness and transform your belief system. It can help you if you choose to love, accept, and embrace yourself just the way you are, which is absolutely perfect. The word *Stalk* may be very frightening to you. You may react negatively to it, thinking, "Oh my goodness, is someone stalking me?" However, if you choose to use the Toltec wisdom presented in this book, you will forget all your old beliefs, including those about stalking, and you will create something new. The art of Stalking—the art of Stalking *yourself*—is a creative, imaginative process that is only about *you;* it is not about anyone else.

The concept of Stalking comes from the cat, who is a master Stalker. If you decide to practice the art of Stalking, you will be the Stalker. As a beginning warrior, you will be a Jaguar Knight, the cat. Stalking will be your beginner's work. You will not be Stalking anyone outside yourself, pointing the finger at others, blaming them for your unhappiness. You will be Stalking yourself: your thoughts, feelings, patterns of behavior, and emotional wounds acquired throughout life. You will be pointing the finger at yourself, looking into your own heart. The doors once closed will start to open, and you will begin to heal all your wounds, one by one, in order that you may live life fully, embracing it for what it is. Stalking will lead you to self-healing and transformation.

The journey to learn Stalking for self-healing and transformation will first take you into the depths of your own belief system. You will learn how the domestication process of the Dream of the Planet alienates you from your true self and from freedom, peace, contentment, and love. In the course of the chapters that follow, you will see how the Judge and the Victim, which are parts of your own personal Parasite, function in your life, perpetuating discontent and the illusion of what "should" be. You will learn about the many "hooks" in life, which grab your attention and make you lose your direction. You will see how your wounds are created by the agreements given to you by others in the Dream. Agreements are the seeds that others plant in you by the power of their words and actions. When you truly believe the agreements, you end up limiting your experiences in life. You are then afraid to live and to express your true self. Instead, you wear a mask that presents to the world what you believe others want to see. You wear a mask to get what you think you want, which you believe will make you happy. Only you never really feel happy. You continue to look for more things and better things, like a better job that pays more money, or a bigger house, or another car, or a better partner. In the process you feel miserable, and you don't know who you really are or what is truly important in life.

The first set of tools to find yourself and manifest your own visions, which consists of the things you want for your life, are the eleven spiritual guidelines listed in chapter 10. Their purpose is to guide you in your everyday life. The Toltec wisdom in this book teaches you to be a warrior, which sounds violent, but the war you are waging is not about violence. Instead, you will love this war because it is about being kind, gentle, and loving with yourself, maybe for the first time in your life. This war is against the parts of the belief system you have internalized and the functions of your own mind such as the Judge. Like most people, you are probably your own worst Judge, always making yourself feel bad. To win this personal war and find peace, you have to make a commitment to yourself and take the next step. The next step is to become a Jaguar Knight and be an apprentice to *yourself*.

Once you make the commitment and apprentice to yourself, you begin the journey and start Stalking, that is, using a powerful tool to assist you in transforming your life. This tool can help you reclaim energy you have lost in living life; experience greater awareness, inner peace, and contentment; and reach a place of feeling unconditional love for yourself and others. It is up to you to take the first step, as well as each step after that. Sometimes it takes great courage and perseverance to face yourself and your truth. If you have the courage and the will to change, then this book can be a tool to help guide you.

2

THE DOMESTICATION
OF YOUR SOUL

The Belief System

THE BELIEF SYSTEM OF THE WORLD, THE DREAM OF THE
Planet, provides the framework for everything you
perceive, and in doing so, impacts what you think, feel,
and believe. When I started doing work on the Toltec
path, one of the first things I learned was how important this belief system of the world was. Since much
of the work I was about to start doing involved this
belief system, I needed to understand what it was,
how it affected me, and what role it played in my unhappiness. The same is true for you: it is important
for you to understand this belief system so that you

will then understand your reasons for choosing to change your life.

Everything in your life, including your search for personal truth and change, takes place within the huge belief system of the Dream of the Planet and its many different levels. Each level holds specific beliefs that manifest as rules, as well as the consequences for not following these rules. You can visualize the Dream of the Planet as circles within circles of belief systems. The belief systems of the larger circles impact those of the smaller circles. The largest circle, the outer one, is the belief system of the government of whatever country you live in. The government has a strong influence on you. It controls you by setting up beliefs through the opinions expressed in official documents, such as the Constitution in the United States. It creates laws, which are the rules you operate by; the consequence for not following them is jail.

Within the first circle is a second circle, which is the belief system of your religion. All religions are belief systems with their own rules and consequences. The beliefs of the religions are transmitted through teachings such as those in the Bible, the Torah, and the Koran. Rules such as the Ten Commandments in the Catholic religion also exist to guide your spiritual life and keep you from going to hell, a consequence of breaking the rules. Religions tend to frame most life choices as either right of wrong. In the Toltec teachings, religion is not seen as bad, or right or wrong. Each religion is seen as just another belief system.

Other circles are the belief systems of your school, and your peers, and the culture in which you were born. Finally, there is the circle with the greatest direct impact on you: the belief system of your family. Your family has its own personal belief system that is based on the larger ones; this system determined how you were brought up as a child. You were taught what was "right" and "wrong" and "good" and "bad" based on the various levels of belief system in which you were raised. The present-day impact of these beliefs that were filtered through your family is tremendous, because, until you choose to create your own Dream, they determine how you feel about yourself every moment in life, as well as what your desires are.

The belief systems of the Dream of the Planet teach you that there are certain things that mean you have a "good" life. You may carry these beliefs in the form of internalized expectations and desires, such as, "I want to have the most beautiful house, with a pretty white fence; my husband is going to be so perfect; I will have beautiful children and they will eat white fluffy bread." Perhaps you grew up in that environment with your parents, and your parents grew up in that environment with their parents. Or maybe your grandparents didn't have white fluffy bread; maybe they had tortillas and sopaipillas like my grandmother and great-grandmother. The details may be different for different people, but the belief systems basically are the same.

The story of one person who studied with me, Rosario, is a typical example of family influence. The Dream would say that she came from a "good" background and had the "perfect" family. But as Rosario was growing up, she saw differences between her parents' actions at home and what they presented to the world, based on their beliefs. She questioned things like the "perfect" marriage and the love between her mother and father. She often saw her father yelling at her mother, throwing clothes, shoes, and other things at her. Even more dramatic were the times her father wanted to, and came close to, killing the kids because he was so angry with his wife. Sometimes Rosario was left locked for hours in a hot car with her sisters while her father went for a drink at the bar. Other times she was trapped in the car as he drove fast down the highway, weaving in and out of traffic. There were many close calls. The children's lives were in jeopardy because her father was so angry with her mother. Rosario would look at her parents and think, "Is this love? Is this a perfect family?"

Rosario's parents believed they needed to have the perfect marriage, and they presented that image to the world, since it had been their world and religion that had told them the perfect marriage was important in the first place. Her parents wanted people to see that they loved each other enough to have eight children. But was their having children really about love? Rosario later realized that, for her father, producing children was a statement of masculinity. Her father's ego and his desire for power and control over her mother manifested in actions that implied, You're my wife, and any time I want to have sex with you, I will, and Don't take the pill because you have to have children. Rosario's mother felt she had to stay home with the kids all the time to be a "good" mother. Meanwhile, her father had complete control and led his own life. Friends of the family saw Rosario's parents as having the "perfect family," but was it really?

The family's idea of perfection continued beyond the relationship of the mother and father and was passed on to the children. The children had to be a certain way too. Rosario went to Catholic school and had a good education. In her Catholic upbringing she was taught that most everything she did was a sin. If she thought about sex it was a sin. If she masturbated in her room it was a mortal sin. Why? Because the belief was that feeling a sexual sensation was wrong, even though it was very human. Rosario felt she had to be a good Catholic and be seen by her family and the world as a good Catholic, so she tried to deny her humanness and how she felt. Since this was so difficult to do, she "sinned" frequently and had to go to confession often.

In Rosario's family there were a number of beliefs that affected the children. When she was a little girl, she lived with her parents, three sisters, and four brothers in a huge, two-story house. In her traditional Spanish family, the belief was that boys did not have to clean or cook. Girls were supposed to clean the house and cook all the meals. So the girls would spend all weekend cleaning the house, shopping for food, and preparing meals, while the boys would go out and have fun. The boys were also bossy, and expected the girls to do whatever they asked them to. Rosario's reaction was, "Boy, you know what, I don't ever want to get married because this is not fair. There is not a balance here. And I definitely don't want to marry anybody like my father or brothers."

Another belief Rosario's family held was that anyone older could tell anyone younger what to do. She was the second youngest of the eight kids, so this belief affected her deeply. Even when she was a grown woman her siblings would tell her what she should and should not be doing. They would say her job wasn't good enough. They would tell her that they thought her partners were too old, or too young, or not in her own culture and therefore not right for her. They believed they had a right to tell Rosario what to do, and she believed she had to listen to them.

After years of living like this, Rosario finally reached the point that it was time to stand up for herself, and she became a warrior. She decided to stop listening to all the opinions and suggestions of her siblings, and she stood up to each one of them with love and truth. She told them that they had no right to tell her who to be or what kind of job to have. Because she spoke her truth, her siblings now respect her incredibly. And Rosario respects them and loves them just the way they are. She does not want to change them—they have to want to change themselves.

Rosario's mom and dad changed as they got older because of their fear of death, which pushed them to reflect on their lives. As a result, they let go of a lot of old beliefs. Now they are happier and more content in life. Rosario's relationship with her parents didn't change, however, until she also stood up to them with her truth.

Now they are more respectful of her, and she just loves and adores them so much. However, it took a long time for Rosario to reach a point of mutual respect with her parents. First, she had to change herself by tackling the beliefs she grew up with.

The Domestication Process

The beliefs you grew up with were powerful. They affected you deeply, because of the domestication process in the Dream of the Planet, through which you learned to believe in and follow the rules set up by the belief systems. You, like everyone else, were domesticated. Your mind was trained from the moment you were born to learn what the rules were, what was right and wrong and good and bad, how to get attention, and how to get what you thought you wanted. You were a good girl or boy when you did something your parents thought was great. You got their attention or a treat. And you were bad when you broke the rules of your parents or the rules of the Dream of the Planet by doing something like stealing candy.

Think about how you domesticate an animal such as a puppy. You feed it, and you give it praise or a treat when it does something you want it to do, like urinating outdoors. You scold the puppy if it messes in the house. The puppy eventually learns the rule—if it urinates outside, it gets what it wants, which is praise and a treat. You then say the puppy is housebroken. Well, simply put, this is how you were domesticated.

Through the domestication process, you were taught the rules of how to live your life. You were taught to obey the rules of society, government, and of course, your mother and father. Your parents believed that what was good for them was supposed to be good for you. The domestication "files" were then stored in your mind and guided you about how to relate to people, how to communicate with people, and how to feel about yourself and others. As an example of domestication let's say that the people in a certain imaginary town are financially well off. Over time, they start believing that they are better people than the poorer individuals who live in a nearby town. They bring up their children with the belief that people get what they deserve in life. They believe that since they are better people, they are rewarded with financial success. They also believe that the people in the other town are not good people and are therefore "punished" by being poor. The children of both towns learn what kind of people they feel comfortable relating to, which are people from the same town they grow up in. The belief they are brought up with and how they are domesticated also determine what kind of wounds they carry in their hearts. For the children in the poor town, this means they may always believe they are unworthy because they are poor.

The Parasite

The Parasite is a function of your mind that develops through the domestication process and is based on the belief system. It is most easily identified as the constant conversation taking place in your mind. This inner "voice" generates all those little words you hear when you are thinking about things or interacting with others. It helps to create and intensify your emotional wounds, and it leads to unhappiness.

The Parasite is with you all the time, in every setting of your life. For example, you're at a party and somebody says something to you. You respond, but then you immediately think that what you said sounded strange and awkward. That thought is your Parasite speaking. You then move on to talk to someone else, but you still feel strange about what you said. You let it go for the moment. However, when you go home and you are all alone, your Parasite kicks in even more strongly. You think to yourself, "Wow, I can't believe I said that. Did I really say that? I'm so embarrassed. What must people think of me? They must think I'm strange." Then you start pro-jecting. You project a scenario onto people in which they are talking about you, and in which they think you have a lot of nerve to say what you said. You have a whole conversation in your mind in which you dive into total judgment of yourself. Before you know it you've made up a whole drama. You think, feeling sad, "How did I even have the nerve to say that? That was the dumbest thing I could have ever said. God I feel so bad I said that." This is your Parasite speaking, and it is just a small ex-ample of what your mind can do. It is an experience you have had before, and it is a process that can become quite extreme.

Another common experience of the Parasite is the following: Imagine you are a wife waiting at home for your husband. You think, "Where's my husband? He hasn't called, and he was supposed to take me out to dinner. He said he was working late." Then the phone rings, and when you answer it somebody hangs up. You think, "Who was that? Is my husband having an affair? Is he seeing some-body else? Maybe that's why he forgot my birthday last month. I'm not even important to him anymore. Yes, there's somebody else. I didn't even think about it before, but now it's making a lot of sense." You build up a huge drama in-side yourself and then respond to it with a lot of negative emotions. And guess what: You don't even know if it's the truth. This is your Parasite.

The Parasite is the master of masters inside you. You created it, and it grows through domestication. It survives by feeding on the emotions taught to you by the domestication process such as sadness, envy, and judgment. It learns how to master your weaknesses and what pushes your buttons. It knows exactly how to shift you to make you react. It creates situations to which you respond on a gut level with anger, jealousy, hurt, or sadness. When you react with such an emotion, you are giving your energy to your Parasite. This energy is eaten by your Parasite, which makes your Parasite stronger. As your life goes on, your Parasite gets stronger and stronger because it continues to eat your emotions, and it continues to create these emotions by creating the situations to which you react.

You may not realize that by reacting to situations with strong emotions, you are feeding the energies of these emotions. When you feed these energies, they expand. They become stronger. As a result, you go deeper into jealousy, sadness, anger, depression, self-pity, and so on every time you react with these emotions.

When you decide that you want to change your life, you have to look at your emotions, your Parasite, and at what maintains the patterns of behavior and the belief structures in your mind. When you become a warrior, you are at war with your Parasite and the beliefs you have taken on through your own personal domestication. You enter into battle to fight the many years of that domestication, in which the same situations and same patterns have come up over and over again. For example, if you are a woman who has found yourself in one abusive relationship after another, when you become a warrior you can choose to look at that pattern and change it. It will not change over night; you will need to continually watch for the Parasite and learn strategies to transform it. And this is not easy, because the Parasite will fight for its survival.

There are two aspects of the Parasite: the Judge and the Victim. These are discussed in the next chapter.

3

THE JUDGE
AND THE VICTIM

The Judge

ONE ASPECT OF THE PARASITE, WHICH IS CREATED THROUGH
the domestication process, is the Judge. It is a master of
telling you what you "should" be doing. Visualize standing before an actual judge or watching a movie with a judge
in it. You will notice that the judge is always observing,
listening to what is being said, noticing reactions that are
occurring, and stating opinions about the proceedings. The
Judge inside you does the same thing: it judges everything
that you do. When your Judge is active, you are constantly
your own hardest critic. You probably judge yourself
harder than any other person in the Dream of the Planet.

The Judge has a job, which is to distinguish between your beliefs and expectations and your actual performance. The belief systems in the Dream of the Planet, and therefore your own belief systems, tell you how to present yourself in life. They tell you that you need to have an image to give to life and to other people. Whenever your image in the Dream of the Planet is challenged, or you feel it is not being accepted, your Judge comes on intensely once you are out of the presence of other people and are alone. For example, perhaps you are a woman who believes it is important to be "good mother," which you define as meaning that you should always be patient with your two-year-old child. Then one day your child screams for three hours. You try everything to soothe him, but you cannot. Finally you lose your patience and scold the child. An hour later, after you calm down, your Judge starts in on you. A little voice in your head starts saying things like, "You are supposed to be a good mother. If you were a good mother, you would not have lost your patience, so you're not a good mother. What would other people think?" and on and on. Then the feelings start to come.

The Judge always brings up feelings such as guilt or shame. For example, after you've been in conversation with other people, your Judge may tell you that you didn't speak the correct words, or that you were too direct or not direct enough, or that you never spoke your truth and just said things so people would accept you. Your feelings may be quite extreme, and you may think, "Why didn't I say something else?" or "Why didn't I do something else?" Those "whys" are your Judge. The Judge is you. When you are being the Judge, you are your own hardest critic.

The Judge can be present every moment of your life and affect your happiness through constant self-judgment. You may not be happy deep down even if you look content and happy to others. A smile on your face doesn't always mean that you are truly happy. Maybe you feel a moment of happiness or contentment when you accomplish something you feel is a great goal in life and the Judge says, "Good" to you. But then the fleeting feeling of accomplishment is gone, and unhappiness creeps back in. So you create another goal to look forward to in life, the Judge saying, "You have to do more next time." True happiness is contentment of the heart and soul no matter what the outcome of any situation. Happiness does not mean that you're laughing constantly and feeling overjoyed. True contentment could express itself as total silence and peacefulness and never having to say one word to anybody.

The Victim

The Victim is another aspect of the Parasite. It is the part of you that says, "Poor me." It comes from wanting a lot of attention and basing everything on how sad your life is when you don't get it. The Victim causes you to want people to feel sorry for you because things aren't going the way you want them to, or the way you feel they "should" go. The Victim is created by the little voice of self-pity in your mind that tells you how you feel about yourself. "Oh, poor me, I didn't get this job and I really deserved it," or "Poor me, my husband left me with all the kids and I'm by myself." The truth is, things just happen in life—and nothing is ever poor for you. This is only what the Victim tells you. You have to assume responsibility and take action when things happen in your life. When you take action and let go of the Victim, the self-pity, and poor me stories, you can look into everything in the Dream of the Planet that is out there to help you. There are laws in the Dream of the Planet that take care of you.

Take the case of Joan. Joan was thirty-nine years old and had two teenage kids. She was in a horrible marriage for twenty years. Her husband was emotionally abusive, had one affair after another, never contributed to the family financially, and was uninvolved with the kids. After many years, Joan finally decided to divorce her husband. At that same time, there were a number of unexpected expenses, including a new car. Joan couldn't pay her rent or other bills and was having problems with the kids. Although she had started to take responsibility and action by getting a divorce, when things got tough she fell into the role of the Victim. She felt sorry for herself and complained to anyone who would listen. Instead, she could have looked into legal options to take care of herself and her kids, such as going to court to get child support. Joan would not confront the father of her children and insist he take responsibility for supporting them. Instead she struggled, trying to borrow money from friends and family. In the process she got a lot of attention from people who felt sorry for her. Joan became the classic Victim. A warrior strives to stop the self-pity, and take action.

The Swing between the Judge and the Victim

Visualize the symbol for Libra, the scales. You are holding the center of the scales: on one side of you is the Judge, and on the other side of you is the Victim. The two sides of the scales swing back and forth. First the Judge slams you so hard with self-judgment that you go into the deepest hole of guilt and shame. Then the balance swings to the opposite side, and you become a Victim filled with self-pity. The scales then shift again and the Judge scolds you for having self-pity and for being a Victim. You point the finger at yourself as a bad person, a sad person, a person who can never do anything right in life. The Judge takes you to the deepest point of feeling that you're not worth anything. You are then the biggest Victim. These are the acts of the Parasite.

4

HOOKS AND MASKS

Hooks

THERE ARE ALWAYS A LOT OF CHALLENGES WHEN YOU look at yourself and your life in order to change. These challenges occur because, as much as you are unhappy and want to change, on some level you may be comfortable with the way things are. Maybe you don't want to look at unpleasant things about yourself, or have a fear of the process, or a fear of what will happen after you change. These feelings arise from the part of you that resists change, and they are made even stronger by the Parasite, which says things like, "Well, things aren't so bad; they could be worse," or, "Other people are the real problem; if only they would change," or, "I am so busy, I don't really have a lot of time." Some of the things in the Dream of the Planet that help your Parasite sabotage your growth process are called hooks. Hooks grab your attention so that you don't have to look at yourself. And when you focus your attention on the hooks, they have the ability to take your happiness.

Visualize hooks. You may see them as fish hooks. When you go fishing, you put a little bait on the tips of the hooks so that you can attract fish. The Dream of the Planet has similar hooks: they contain bait, and the fish they attract is you. These hooks are everything around you that takes your attention and keeps you entertained long enough that you don't have to look at yourself. Some examples of hooks are the thousands of different kinds of foods, restaurants, concerts, music, clothes, and "neon lights" in your life. And just so that you never get bored and shift your attention, the industries that create these hooks change their products very quickly. Music, electronics, computers, and fashion change every moment. The belief system of the Dream of the Planet tells you that you have to have the latest, greatest "things" to be accepted.

You may want your neighbors to look at what you have. For example, you may drive a luxury car so that your neighbors can see how well you are doing. At the same time, however, a particular neighbor may envy you.

He may wonder how you can afford that car when he can't buy one and you both have the same kind of job. So he then has to purchase something for you to envy. You then engage in a constant battle to look better than the person next to you, and all of your focus and energy goes into this competition.

If you take this battle to the next level, you become completely lost in everything that exists in the Dream as you battle to keep up with the things you want. You work two or three jobs in order to afford your dream car and dream home. You work so hard you have no time to enjoy them, and money is so tight there is none left over for anything else. You may have the most incredible home, car, and job, but these things are still not enough. You want more—you want better things and a higher position at work. And the whole time, you are not happy or content in life. The hooks are eating you up.

Money is one of the biggest hooks for most people in the Dream of the Planet. You may be hooked either by wanting to have enough of it or by your reaction to having to "give it away." You may believe you have enough. Maybe you enjoy working. You have fun and make good money at the same time. But then you still have to pay the government for your fun because you owe taxes. Having to pay the government a huge chunk of money can take away your happiness. As a warrior, you have to work on letting that tax money go. Money is a gift from the universe—it is not what makes you happy.

One of the other biggest hooks is relationships. Relationships in the Dream of the Planet reflect how women and men believe they have to be in life. The media shows men how to be manly. Television and advertising show women how to look beautiful and what they need to do to attract men. From this perspective, being in a relationship is everything. Women often define their self-worth by being in relationships. If they are not married or attached, they feel like they are not desirable or good enough.

Depending on the environment and culture you were brought up in, you probably hold certain expectations about marriage. If you are a woman, you may feel that marriage elevates your status and earns you a level of respect, especially from the members of your culture and your spiritual group, your church, temple, or other affiliation. If you are a man, you may feel that you are more respected in the business and political world if you are married. You may even ignore how you are treated in your relationship, believing that if you are totally abused, ignored, or neglected, you are still supposed to stay in your marriage. Perhaps you believe this because you gave your vows to God in a certain ceremony, or because you fear losing the respect of your church or community. Or you may stay in the relationship to keep up an image, basing your decision on how it looks to others. You may think that if you leave your relationship, you will be seen as a failure in the eyes of the Dream and will now be less desirable because you are single (translate "unwanted"). So you end up stuck in an abusive pattern, losing your sense of self-worth to maintain the relationship.

Masks

Some of the other things in the Dream of the Planet that help your Parasite sabotage your growth process are called masks. Masks are things you put on your face so people can't tell who you are. You look different—like the masks you put on. You may put on masks every day; there are millions of masks in the Dream. Masks are the different faces you wear, the different statements you make to the Dream of the Planet to tell others who you are—only these faces are not who you truly are underneath the masks. For example, you may put on a mask to say that you're very intelligent, or that you're the greatest artist that exists, yet deep down you may not feel that way. You may be very insecure. The Parasite tells you that you need to put on the masks so that people will like or accept you, and you will get what it is you want.

You, like every human being, become a master of the mask, but it is not the mask of sincerity or impeccability. It is whatever mask you believe will get you what you think you want. Ultimately you pay a price in life for wearing the masks. Learning to wear masks begins in childhood, through the domestication process. This is how children become such good manipulators. When you were a child, you realized that if you put on a certain mask, you could get what you wanted in life. Your mask may have been being cute, the good girl/boy, the funny child, the tough guy, or any number of other possibilities. You quickly learned which masks worked for you. As you grew into an adult, you learned to wear more and more masks and to become masterful at them.

Saying that you are a great lover is one of the biggest masks in the Dream of the Planet. And sex, like relationships, is one of the biggest hooks. You may want to be lovers with someone desirable in the Dream and then walk away and say, "I not only had this special person, but I was the greatest lover they ever had." Another big mask is the mask of wealth. You may want to wear the mask that you are wealthy by driving an expensive car, living in an expensive house, or wearing designer clothes. These may be way above your budget, but you buy them just to look like you have money or are well off.

You have so many masks that are part of your everyday life because the masks keep you from having to look at your true self. Putting on a mask is as simple and routine as deciding which dress or suit you are going to wear that day. One of the most common masks is the one you wear around your friends. You decide every day whether you are sincere around them or whether you are going to be fake, putting on a mask so you will be liked and accepted. Not only children and high school kids do this.

You put on masks regardless of your church, your environment, or your culture. As an adult, you put on masks to get the greatest partner, to be looked up to by members of your culture or community, and to be accepted in whatever social circle you try to be in. You change masks like you're changing your clothes. You get so lost in the separation of yourself from your true nature that you never look at your soul. Meanwhile, you feel empty and sad inside, and are always searching for something to fill the emptiness.

When you become a warrior, you put the masks away. The veils behind which you have hidden fall away. As a warrior, you face the fear of looking at your true self with all your wounds and hurt. You face the abuse by your father or mother and work toward embracing yourself when you feel sadness, pain, or any other emotion. You talk about and face the reality of your life, no matter how "bad" it is in the eyes of the Dream of the Planet. For example, suppose you are a heroin addict who has sold drugs to others who have died. When you become a warrior, you are able to drop the tough, cool mask of indifference to others' pain and death. You accept responsibility for your actions, but you do not judge yourself. You look at your woundedness and embrace yourself. You let go of each of your masks and love your true being. That is the beginning of breaking the masks of the belief system.

This first step in breaking the masks of the belief system involves becoming a Jaguar Knight. However, becoming a Jaguar Knight involves wearing a mask too. It is a mask that helps you break all the other masks you have created. When you put on the mask of the Jaguar Knight you look through the Jaguar's eyes, not through the eyes of self-pity or seduction. You become the jaguar and watch yourself every moment. You are patient with yourself when you hunt the emotions inside you that keep you stuck. You participate in the gradual, gentle process of releasing. Once you break all your masks, you are totally new. You see yourself freely, clearly, and in total honesty. Then you can dance and walk down the street with yourself, and truly like who you are. You are separate from the Dream of the Planet's belief system. You have your own belief, which is to love everything that exists and feel peace in your heart.

5

AGREEMENTS

The Seeds of Behavior

AGREEMENTS ARE BELIEFS THAT CONTRIBUTE TO WHAT you think and how you feel about yourself. They are given to you, usually as a child, while you are being domesticated. Through the domestication process, your parents, family, culture, church, and other authority figures give you the same agreements given to them by similar figures in their own lives. These agreements are given in the form of words and actions. These words and actions teach you how to live and love. They offer opinions on right and wrong based on what the givers believe is truth for them. Once you take in an agreement, it affects what you think, feel, and do. A pattern of behavior develops around the agreement. This process in turn strengthens the agreement and builds a "tunnel" of similar experiences over time.

Agreements have been given to women for generations and generations through the teachings of the church. They go back to the story of Adam and Eve. Eve was created from Adam's rib as a servant for him. She was also weaker spiritually, acted against God's wishes, and was to blame for Adam's temptation and fall from grace. When Eve gave Adam the forbidden apple, she created all the suffering that happened in the Dream after that. Some of the agreements passed on to women from this story are: women are servants for men; women are to blame when something bad happens in the Dream; and women will always suffer in life.

Visualize the generational chain reactions arising from the agreements of Adam and Eve. These agreements have continued to the present day, with variations in different religions and belief systems. The agreements extend beyond religion and family to many areas of life, including politics. In previous generations, women could never participate in politics. Now women are taking action and choosing differently, but that has only occurred in the past sixty years or so.

The Altar Girl

The following story illustrates how an agreement works. It is about a little girl who was nine years old and had a very deep agreement enter her life. This little girl was brought up in the Catholic Church and always went to mass. She loved going to church with her mother and father and family on Sundays. Every week she would watch her brother work as an altar boy. She liked what he did, so she wanted very much to be an altar girl, but at the time she was growing up there was no such thing. Girls and women were not allowed on the altar except to clean, and that was only when there was no mass and nobody in the church. But the little girl did not know this.

So one day the little girl said to her mother after mass, "Mom, I want to serve God. I want to be an altar girl. I want to be on the altar serving the priest." Her mother said, "Oh sweetheart, there are only altar boys. They don't have altar girls. Girls are not allowed to serve on the altar." The little girl replied, "But Mom, I really want to serve. Can we ask the priest and let him know I want to serve?" Her mom said, "Have you seen any altar girls serving? No. Have you ever seen any girls on the altar? No. Well there's your answer. Why is the priest going to let you start serving all of a sudden when they don't allow women on the altar?" The little girl persisted, saying, "But why, Mom, why? I would do my best. I want to serve God. I want to be the best for God." Her mom replied, "Only boys and men are allowed to serve God in that way. Only men are allowed to be priests. Girls serve their brothers and fathers, and women serve their husbands. Women take care of the home and have children." Based on this conversation, the little girl took in the agreement from her mother that men and boys were automatically more special. Because they could serve God on the altar, they were elevated to positions of authority and power in life.

Although the little girl was unaware of this agreement that she took in from her parents and culture, in her day-to-day life she experienced the pattern of this agreement in action. Men were always the religious leaders, the spiritual advisers with the spiritual answers. Men were also the political leaders, philosophers, artists, and just about everything else powerful. However, women as mothers and housewives with little or no power were trained to take whatever was given to them.

This agreement about men's authority and power continued to have a huge impact on the little girl's behavior. It shaped the day-to-day events, such as her not speaking up in class to disagree with boys, as well as the bigger events. In high school, she wanted to run for president of the student council. But she chose not to do so because she believed that boys were really the political leaders. It would have taken a lot of courage for her to run for office since she would have been the only girl running against boys, but she was not ready to fight the huge system of beliefs, both within herself and around her.

Everything in life was more challenging for this little girl because her spirit was huge, and deep down inside her she knew she wanted to be a leader. She had the energy to be a leader and to serve God. As she got older, she realized that her energy, desire, and love were no different than a man's and that perhaps her feelings were even more sincere. She had held back her intense spirit— a spirit that wanted to serve in every way. As she became a young woman, she realized that following the beliefs of the Dream went against how she felt about herself and her role in life, causing her unhappiness and discontent.

So this young woman became a warrior in order to connect with her true spirit and find happiness. She understood that she had to look at her belief system and find the agreements deep down inside her that were holding her back. As a warrior, she started to Stalk her life patterns in order to find and break these agreements. She wanted to become content. When she started this process, she felt she didn't fully understand what it meant to Stalk since she had never done anything like it before, but deep down inside her she knew it would help her.

The woman discovered that there were many agreements in her life, and that each one had created its own tunnel of energy over time. These tunnels needed to be cleaned. However, she also knew that she was unaware of most of the agreements she had taken in and how the patterns affected her. Her ultimate goal was to trace the patterns back to their source—to discover the original agreements behind them. This involved cleaning the tunnels as she went, and then breaking the agreements once they were found.

The young woman began with the present day and started to look at her life. She saw that her role as a woman was different from that of a man. This was reflected everywhere around her. At gatherings, she and the other women, but not the men, would get the drinks and prepare the food. Repairmen didn't take her seriously; they always asked to speak to her husband. The young woman saw that, in her life, men were authority figures in positions of power, while women were domesticated to be of service to men.

The young woman looked at her marriage and job situation in her day-to-day life. She realized that she worked because she "had to," but that she had never loved her job or seen it as a career—a way for her to grow. She also realized that she was married because it was expected of women, and that her role as a wife for her husband came before her job. The young woman felt the leader inside her wanting to express itself; she realized that she wanted a career, not a job, and that if she did not pursue a career she was going against her true spirit. She also felt that, although she loved her husband, she wanted an equal relationship with him, not one in which she was a servant.

As the young woman continued to look backward in time at the patterns in her life, certain events stood out to her. She remembered graduating from high school and dating the man she eventually married. At that time, she had several talks with her parents about her future. She wanted to go to college like her brothers and work with the church to serve God, but because she was a woman, her parents told her she needed to get married and raise a family. Even though she felt a heavy feeling inside her when she discussed this with her parents, she agreed to get married. Her mother told her, "He is such a nice man, a good catch. You'll have such beautiful children."

The agreement associated with this pattern of behavior started to enter the young woman's awareness as she reflected on this memory. She saw how she had held herself back because she was a woman, and how she had perceived men as having the authority and power in life. So she continued looking at her life. She remembered high school and how she had wanted to run for student council. She continued going back in time, remembering similar events. Finally, she saw the original agreement, which was given to her the day she told her mother she wanted to become an altar girl.

At this point, the young woman chose to break this agreement she had accepted as a young girl. In doing so, she realized that not only was she helping herself, but she was becoming a leader for other women, as she had been brought into this world to do. She was opening a door to change the way the belief system had always been. She saw that she was here to help change old agreements. She saw that she was here to help change the agreements given to little girls by society and religions. Her path was to show women that they are special, that they can be healers, powerful politicians, and anything else that men can be. She had learned that the inner courage to step forward in life was the power to change old beliefs and transform.

This story of the altar girl is an example of how one agreement can deeply affect your life. You have taken in many, many agreements, some more intense than others. These agreements usually create emotional wounds and, as described earlier, affect your behavior by creating patterns. For the would-be altar girl, the pattern was always feeling not good enough. If you do not look at your agreements and heal your wounds, the patterns of your behavior will continue and be passed on to your children.

The Abused Child

Another example of a huge agreement that creates a very deep wound is the experience of sexual abuse. If as a child you were sexually abused by a parent, and later you do not look at the wound of this agreement and heal it, you will continue the pattern of being in abusive relationships throughout your life. You will probably marry someone who was also abused, and the pattern will be passed on to your children. The intent of this work is to break such a pattern by finding and looking at the agreement behind it, and then healing the wound.

When you are abused as a child, you learn many agreements related to the abuse. You learn that there are no boundaries between yourself and others. You learn that you can't say no to others, since in abuse there is no place for "no." Your parent (or other trusted person), the most important teacher in your life, has no respect and crosses your physical and emotional boundaries. As a child, you cannot say no to the person who is the main authority figure in your life, whom you love and trust, but also whom you fear the most. Some common agreements that you take in as an abused child are: you cannot say no; it is okay for others to cross your boundaries, and okay for you to cross the boundaries of others; it is okay for people you love and trust to hurt you; you are powerless to protect yourself; and you have no self-worth.

You will grow up and, until these agreements are found and healed, you will go from relationship to relationship with abusive partners, or stay in a particular abusive relationship, until you choose to look inside at your emotional wounds. You must look at all the emotions occurring at every moment of your life. You may have many emotions, and much sadness and unhappiness, yet you may have no idea where the feelings are coming from. You have to start going into your life, looking inside your heart to see what created this pattern. You may not know why you are unhappy. You may not remember the abuse, or connect your emotions to it. Doing so can be a long process.

The process of healing is not about judging the person who gave you the agreements or abused you. At first, of course, you'll have anger and other emotions when you come to realize the root of your unhappiness. But the intent is to clean the tunnels of the agreements—to embrace and heal your wounds—until you get to a place where there isn't anger anymore; you realize that the situation just was. Then nothing can ever take your happiness again. No matter what your situation, you have contentment in your heart, because you have worked for that contentment. You have worked to look at the wounds and feel the sadness and experience the shock of whatever is truth for you, and you have worked to heal all of it.

Healing means reaching the point that your price— your self-worth—is much higher. Then you put yourself on a pedestal. You respect, love, and treat yourself as you would the highest queen or king. You have tremendous love for your own personal body, spirit, and soul. When you change the agreements, the vibration of your own personal ray of light, your energy field, starts to shift. You start letting the poison out of your system, and you become so much more radiant. With the poison gone, there is room for loving yourself. And when you love yourself, your actions reflect that love. Instead of choosing an abusive partner, you choose a partner who has done spiritual or other personal growth work in his or her life, and with whom you can communicate truthfully. Your partner in turn can communicate truthfully with you. Your partner's intent, like your own, is to not fall into old patterns. You take care of and do the things for yourself that you would want your partner to do for you, since you are your own greatest partner. And of your partner you have no expectations. You simply love and enjoy each other.

6

EDUARDO

Cultural Reflections

THE FOLLOWING STORY DEMONSTRATES HOW THE JUDGE, the Victim, agreements, hooks, and masks work in everyday life. It is about a man who studied with me for a number of years; his name was Eduardo. Eduardo was forty years old and had been brought up with the beliefs and cultural values of a traditional Spanish family. He worked hard for many years, doing everything that the Dream of the Planet told him to do in order to get ahead. Eduardo went to college, got good grades, went on to get a Master's degree, took jobs in which he could move up, met the right people, and so on. One day he was up for a promotion, which would mean a better position in the company he was working for. He did everything he could to get it.

The promotion was a hook for Eduardo. He wanted it badly, and focused all his attention on it. He thought, "What can I do to get that position? How can I present myself to be the best person for that position?" The new job hooked him because it was a step up from his current job. It would look better on his résumé. People would respect him more in the Dream of the Planet. It had higher status. He would be more accepted and feel that he had made it. His wife would think more highly of him because he would be making more money and the family wouldn't be as financially strained. The only problem was that somebody else from a different culture, John, was trying to get the same promotion. And John intimidated Eduardo.

In our destiny cycle and path of spiritual growth in life we are presented every moment with the fears we have inside us. Eduardo was brought up in a culture that taught him to believe he was always in competition with John's culture. His biggest fear and challenge in life was to be compared to and compete with a person like John from the other culture. So of course, at this moment in his life, it was Eduardo's destiny to compete with John, a person from the other culture.

Eduardo went to work early the day the boss was going to make his decision. While waiting to hear the outcome, he felt a little fear and shakiness. But he didn't want others to see how he felt, so he put on a mask that he was confident and happy. Then Eduardo went to talk to his boss, who was also from John's culture. His boss told him, "Well, it was a difficult decision. You've worked hard and done great work. We value you in your current position in the company, but John has been working a little bit longer, and he deserves the promotion at this time. You will be up for something very soon."

Eduardo walked out of his boss's office upset and angry. However, he put on a mask to appear happy for John so that he could congratulate him, even though deep down in his heart he didn't feel happy for John. He really felt like slugging him. His stomach and whole being were enraged. But to be mature in the Dream of the Planet was to go up to John, say congratulations, and walk away.

With his coworkers, Eduardo wore the mask that he was not upset or worried about losing the promotion. One by one they came up to him and said, "Sorry, Eduardo, it's too bad you didn't get the position." He replied to each of them, "Not a big deal. Something else will come up for me." He put on this mask to say that everything was working out all right for him. But once again, deep down in Eduardo's heart, this was not his truth. Eduardo's truth was that he was really upset. He was experiencing all the emotions that had built up inside him since he was a little boy about being compared to individuals from the other culture. Not getting the promotion set off the emotions, which had reached a peak. However, the little voice inside his mind, which was the Judge, kept telling him what he should do, which was to congratulate John, and how he should feel, which was to be happy for John and okay in front of his coworkers.

After work, Eduardo had a few beers. To himself he thought, "Hey, why didn't I get that job?" The Judge came in and hit him over the head, telling him that he was not worthy enough to get the job. Then the cycle of the Victim began. Eduardo experienced self-pity. He felt "poor me." He thought, "How come not me?" He wondered, "Why wasn't I worthy enough to get that job?" He felt that it was because he was born into his Spanish culture and upbringing. After a few drinks, his thinking shifted even more, and the self-pity deepened. He thought, "Damn, I was brought up in a poor environment and worked hard all my life. I did the best I could, and look, I didn't get the job." Eduardo left the bar and went home. The Judge and the Victim had made him miserable; he was very upset. He avoided his children and automatically took out his unhappiness on his wife. He criticized her for everything that evening, treating her like she was worthless because he was feeling worthless himself.

A Closer Look at Eduardo's Beliefs and Agreements

One of the agreements that Eduardo took on during his childhood was that this other culture was better than his. He learned that members of the other culture were his competitors in life, they would always be the best, and that he would always have to compete against them by working extra hard. Eduardo believed this with every breath he took. So he became educated and did everything he could to compete with them, and guess what? When a situation came up in which he went head to head with someone from the other culture, that person beat him. Why? Because the belief system given to him by his family and culture said that the competitor from the other culture was better. As a result, Eduardo felt that he wasn't good enough.

Eduardo needed to work on breaking the agreement of not being as good as members of the other culture. Otherwise he would continue through life disliking them because of how he felt. He would also find that the same competitive situations would keep coming up in his life, deepening the agreement, his unhappiness, and his low self-worth.

When Eduardo became a warrior, he focused instead on breaking the agreements he had in his life. He came to a point where he knew that the only competition that existed was in his own mind. Once he broke all the agreements he had taken on, he was no longer limited by them; there was no fear or doubt if he had been a warrior at the time of his potential promotion, he would have gotten the job if he had truly wanted it deep down in his heart. Or, in not getting it, he would have known that all situations are great opportunities. For Eduardo, this realization did not manifest until he had studied for many years.

7

MIRRORS AND THE EXCHANGE OF ENERGY

Mirrors

As a human being living in the Dream of the Planet, your life centers around other people from the moment you are born. You interact and exchange energy with others constantly, serving as a mirror for others to see themselves, while others serve as mirrors for you. The exchange of energy is the foundation for Stalking, and mirrors enlighten and guide what you are Stalking.

Your purpose is to be present every moment for the cycle of your soul, a process that involves thousands of lifetimes. Everything—every situation that is presented to you in this life—has been there in previous lifetimes.

Every environment, with its trees, stones, buildings, and people, has been part of your life in past lifetimes. Everything in your life is a mirror that is being presented to your once again to see how you will act or react in this lifetime, and thus provide you with an opportunity for spiritual growth.

Everything in your life is a reflection of you. Everything you see around you comes from your own eyes, your own perceptions, and your own emotions. Whatever emotions you feel are your own emotions, not those of the person next to you. No other person makes you react or feel emotions. You might point your finger at others and say they are angry or they are making you mad. But the truth is that your feelings are really about you; the mirrors are reflecting your feelings back to you. When you look into a mirror and see yourself combing your hair, the mirror is not combing your hair; you are combing your hair, and this is being reflected in the mirror. Everything in your life reflects back to you how you see your life and present yourself.

There are mirrors in every interaction. Whatever you don't like about your boss is really a reflection of something you don't like about yourself. You find yourself in that relationship because you and your boss are meant to be together. There is a set of dynamics, a pattern of interacting, that has to be cleared up between the two of you from a past life. Every situation in your life contains something that you have to look at. The key is to have enough awareness not to get hooked into other people's energy fields. Not getting hooked means not reacting to life situations. This takes awareness and being content with yourself. If you get hooked and react to other people, the emotional patterns will continue from experience to experience in this and future lifetimes.

Think about the last time your boss or some other significant person said harsh words to you. Did you react to those words, as you possibly did in past lifetimes, by becoming quiet and feeling bad about yourself? Or did you have the awareness to shift your reaction and allow for the growth of your soul by speaking up and asking in a detached fashion why he or she was being unreasonable? If you didn't react and you stayed detached, you were mastering yourself. When you master yourself, you fall in love with yourself. You are gentle, you have enough awareness to shift yourself from whatever situation is presented to you. You can walk out of the situation and not say or do something that doesn't feel good to you. You can be in the situation and speak your truth and have balance. When you master yourself, you clean the mirrors that are presented to you in life.

When you are a warrior, your intention is to clean the mirror of your life, which is the mirror of your soul. This process begins when you become the Judge or the Victim and you find yourself living within the beliefs and agreements that are given to you. You have to experience these agreements to start shifting and cleaning the mirror. Every experience that you've had in other lifetimes is presented to you in this lifetime over and over again until it is clean in the mirror, and you are content and peaceful with it. That means you have no reaction to it. Instead, you just have love and respect for yourself. When you have love and respect for yourself, you become a mirror of love and respect for others who present themselves to you, including alcoholics, prostitutes, and murderers. You find peace in whatever life brings you, in every moment.

The purpose of your life is your soul, but everything in life doesn't teach you to be aware of your soul. Life teaches you to be aware of how intelligent you are, and of your career status. Yes, it is good to live your life 100 percent and have abundance. But you do not need to be the Victim of wanting everything because you have self-pity and you want people to respect you. Once you respect yourself, everything is there for you.

Eduardo had an agreement that people from the other

culture would always be better, so he had to work extra hard to try and overcome that belief. In a previous lifetime, he experienced the people from the other culture always being better. So every person who was part of that previous lifetime was being encountered once again in this lifetime's Dream. His mirror reflected his biggest fear, which was that people from the other culture worked harder and always got what they wanted. Eduardo had to face his fear by losing the promotion to such a person. He believed he wasn't worthy enough. He had to feel all the related emotions in order to come to the realization that everything he disliked and judged about the person was what he disliked and judged about himself.

The Exchange of Energy

Everything in life is an energy form that has its own personal ray of light from the Source, which some people call God. Trees, plants, rocks, fish, birds, bugs, animals, human beings, and so on all have unique rays of light. As a human being, your energy form is egg shaped, and the amount of energy you have determines the size of your energy field. The more energy you have, the more awareness you have. Awareness helps you take responsibility for transforming each action in life. Doing so increases your energy field. As warrior, you work toward increasing your awareness by reclaiming the energy you have lost in energy exchanges.

Every moment in life you are exchanging energy through your breath, which is energy, and through your actions. When you eat an apple, you are exchanging energy between the food and your body. When you are singing, you are exchanging energy with sound, formed by the breath of life, and with your body. When you interact with others you are exchanging energy through your breath, through the power of your words, and through your actions. Even if for one moment you see the woman who cleans the offices at your work, you are exchanging energy with her. Her energy becomes part of your energy and vice versa. Energy is lost, however, when you become hooked into someone's energy field through an emotional reaction and interaction.

For example, say you are a wife arguing with your husband. The act of arguing is an exchange of energy through your breath and the power of your words. You each speak strong words to each other. The argument arises from the domestication of the belief system that tells you how the relationship is supposed to be, and causes you to have certain expectations of each other. When those expectations are not filled, you argue. For example, you as the wife may not have dinner on the table when your husband gets home from work, so he gets angry and starts an argument with you. The domestication inside each of your minds creates emotions. This occurs because of agreements that were given to you that are now inside you.

The agreement your husband carries from his up-bringing is that wives are supposed to respect and serve their husbands. When you don't serve him dinner, it means you are being disrespectful, and his emotional response is anger. Agreements are always pushed into action by the reflecting mirrors of other people. Mirrors always reflect when they are not clean. Your husband reacts and feels you are not respectful because he does not respect himself. If he did, he would see that you are too exhausted to make dinner because you've had a particularly hard day at home with your five sick kids. The situation has nothing to do with you not respecting your husband, but he still reacts. His reaction to you then pushes your buttons; you then feel inadequate as a wife. When someone pushes your buttons, there is always an exchange of energy.

You know you are hooked and are reacting in an emotional exchange of energy when you feel very drained by an interaction. The other person pulls you in. You and your husband already have an emotional attachment. So when you argue, it is very emotionally draining because there is an exchange of energy thrown around with the power of your words.

Your husband may express the power of his words with a tremendous amount of anger. The feeling of anger is so overwhelming inside his body that he automatically wants to give the emotion or buildup of energy to you, because you are the other part of the exchange. So he starts yelling at you. A tremendous amount of energy is thrown at you. He wants you to react. He is reacting fully and is feeling upset. You in turn are likely to react to his words. When you react, you are hooked. You eat his emotions. You are hooked emotionally through the power of his words and his emotions. He wants to hook you so he can release what he is feeling. He feels better once you eat his anger.

Then the emotion builds up in you, and you want to return it. So you say something to which he reacts, eating your emotions. You feel better, but he feels the emotional buildup again. Your husband then has to say something that hooks you even more strongly so that you will react once again. You each find relief only when the other one reacts. This is the exchange of anger, or any emotion, in an argument.

Sometimes there isn't a mutual exchange of energy. For example, your husband may throw energy at you, and you may just eat it. You may be very passive and have a fear of speaking up, so you go against yourself and take in all the anger that is being thrown at you by your husband. Perhaps you have a fear of speaking up because your husband is emotionally and physically abusive toward you. He might hit you if you speak your truth, and he might hit you if you don't. There is a total emotional and physical drain on you because you take in your husband's anger plus the abuse. You feel exhausted afterward. And, on top of it all, you feel you deserve it. You live your life believing that this is what love is. It is a pattern you saw with your parents, who were taught this pattern by their parents. It is the only way you know how to be in love with somebody and how to treat somebody you feel something for. It is your expression of love, and the belief system of agreements that's deep inside you.

Relationships are the biggest hooks, and where the strongest emotions are expressed. Family is another area where strong emotions are exchanged. So for you as a warrior, relationships and family are your biggest challenges. Your intent as a warrior is to transform the emotions when other people are reacting, and to not react yourself. But you do not want to go against yourself by suppressing your emotions. You just don't want to get hooked into other people's energy fields and then feel like reacting. You want to feel content with yourself. You want to have enough awareness that you can walk away and shift the pattern of energy exchange from the way you've previously experienced it. Once you shift that pattern, the other people have to take responsibility for their actions, and for working through their own emotions.

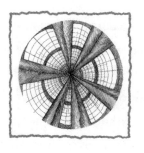

8

MARY

Cycles of Attraction

RECALL THAT YOUR FIRST IMAGES IN LIFE WERE THOSE OF your parents or guardians, and of how you were brought up by them. These people were your first teachers in life. As a child learning how to live in this world, to survive, to trust, to love, to speak, you had nothing else but your caretakers. You gave your whole life to them, although you really had no choice in that role because you were just forming and were completely dependent on them.

Mary's childhood experiences, which included abuse, led to certain beliefs, agreements, judgments, and Victim patterns in her relationships. She was born into a family that had a mother and father who worked very hard in life. They had good jobs and were middle-class people. Mary had all the things she wanted and that seemed important for every child to have: nice toys, tennis shoes, Nintendo games, and everything she saw on television. She loved and trusted her parents completely and, like all children, took in the agreements that were given to her by them. And Mary took on one of the biggest agreements a parent could give a child: the agreement of abuse.

When Mary was very young, about seven years old, she was growing, having fun, and enjoying life. Then one night when she was sleeping in her room, her father came in very quietly. As he got into bed with her, she woke up. Her father of course told her not to say anything and not to make any noise. He said that she was very special to him, that he loved her, that he was there to protect her, and that nothing would harm her. He got very close to her and then suddenly slipped his hand under her panties and touched her vagina. Mary was shocked and didn't know how to respond. Inside her being she knew there was something wrong with what was happening, but she didn't know exactly where to draw the line with her parent. She loved her father and liked to feel special, but she was very afraid. Something was happening emotionally and with her body that was very uncomfortable.

Mary's father continued to talk to her, telling her that Mommy would be mad at her if she found out because she would be jealous and not understand; Mommy would then make Daddy send Mary away. Mary started to worry that her Mommy wouldn't love her anymore if she knew what was happening. Mary thought she would be sent away. Then she would lose both her parents, whom she loved very much.

It didn't take long before Mary's father was going to her room almost every night. This relationship became very painful and sad for Mary. What they did was a big secret. Her father told her that this was what daddies did, and that it was their secret. Daddies loved their daughters so much that they got to hold and love them in a sexual way. So Mary began to think that what her father was doing to her was love. He was "loving" her. Mary wondered if her daddy "loved" her mommy the same way.

Mary's life changed; she was not happy anymore. She walked through life more seriously. As she grew, her beliefs about being a little girl were formed around the abuse. She developed agreements: "People that I trust and are close to me hurt me. Something bad will happen to me if I tell the truth. I can't say what I really feel. I have to protect my father. Love is physical. Love is hurtful. I can't say no." She wondered where trust and truth began. And how she should define the love between her mother and her father, between herself and her father. She knew there was something very, very sad in her heart.

The abuse continued for many years, and Mary became a miserable little girl. She broke all the rules her parents gave her. She hated her mother, who was never there to protect her. She learned to manipulate her father. She became a Victim. She was very wounded and trusted no one. The sacred trust that she had once experienced with her mother and father had been violated, so now she never felt safe or complete. The Judge inside her told her that the abuse was her fault because she "asked" for it. She liked the attention; it made her feel special. Then the Victim inside her told her that she was just a poor little girl who was scared, had nobody to run to for help, had no one to talk to, and felt very sad inside.

In the eyes of the Dream of the Planet, Mary appeared to have a great life. She had all the material things she wanted. As she got older she had a car, designer clothes, and so on. But in her heart she was still so, so sad. The hurt was way deep down inside her. What Mary really wanted was the attention of her mother and father in a nonsexual way, but she never got it. Being sexual was the only way she knew to get the attention she craved. So in high school she was loose with boys and had casual sex with anyone who paid attention to her. She didn't have many girlfriends, and none who were really close. She didn't share her feelings about her father's abuse with anybody. She felt empty inside, like she was living a lie, but she also didn't really know what her truth was.

As a young adult Mary picked guys who treated her badly and wanted to be with her just to fulfill their sexual desires. They never saw her as a serious girlfriend—just something on the side for pleasure. She didn't develop any serious relationships and didn't know how to communicate with men. Sex was her only form of communication. Mary felt a huge need in life, which was to be accepted and liked. She felt this because she never liked herself. And she never even came close to loving herself. She felt shame about the way men used her but she was unable to change the pattern. The roots of Mary's shame lay in her harsh judgment of herself about being with her father. She felt it was her fault.

Later in life Mary met a man named Bob who had great masks that hooked her attention. He was very charming and fun to be with. Even though Mary was a beautiful young woman, she was hooked easily because her wounds made her feel so desperate. Like Mary, Bob was also deeply wounded. He came from the same kind of abusive family background as Mary. This similarity in their backgrounds was no surprise.

The energy that is drawn to you is the same as the energy of the wounds you carry, which you project outward in life. You attract people with similar energies. You magnetize each other and fall in love. Then you are faced with the same patterns and beliefs you were brought up with, and the cycle begins all over again.

Being pulled to somebody involves two things: attraction, and a sensation in your physical body in response to the person. And of course everybody is pulled to somebody. The particular vibration of energy (or ray of light) is the sensation you feel, and the mirror is the attraction you feel. The mirror is the form you see, the person's appearance, although that is really energy too. There are a lot of mirrors, or people that were brought up in the same environment as you and therefore have the same energetic field. However, when a mirror is combined with a physical feeling for someone, the result is a sense of being connected to a person or "chemistry." You may crave the "perfect" chemistry in the form of your "soulmate."

Mary and Bob felt a special chemistry. They got engaged after one month, and married three months later. On the surface, Bob was considered by the Dream of the Planet to be a good husband; he worked hard and Mary had everything she needed. However, shortly after they were married, her husband dropped his masks. Mary then realized that this man was not the person she had met, who had hooked her into taking the step of marriage. He had told her all the things she had wanted to hear just to hook her, and they had all been lies. Now that he was married, Bob was not charming or light-hearted anymore. He was moody and quiet all of the time. The things they had shared during courtship no longer interested him. Mary suddenly felt that she didn't really know Bob—that he was a stranger. They argued all the time, exchanging energy as described earlier.

Unexpectedly, Mary got pregnant and had a child. Although she was very unhappy, she felt that she needed to stay in the marriage and work it out because of the agreements given to her by the church and her family. These agreements said that marriage is for life, divorce is a sin, and parents must stay together for their children. So Mary stuck the marriage out. She and Bob became more distant from each other, and their relationship became filled with problems. Bob got closer and closer to their daughter, and father and daughter developed a "special" closeness. The daughter became Daddy's little girl. By the time she was about seven, she was experiencing the same pattern that had existed in her mother's life. Bob was molesting her in the same way that both he and Mary had been abused as children.

As Mary got older, she became tired of feeling miserable. She tried counseling with her priest, antidepressants, and years and years of psychotherapy. Although each helped her in some way, nothing removed the sadness from her heart. This feeling became so extreme that she was desperate. However, part of her knew that there was something more in life, something beyond her sadness. After searching for alternative ways to help herself, she encountered the Toltec work and began taking action. She began the process of healing her sadness and other emotional wounds.

First Steps Toward Awareness

Once she was on the path of the warrior, Mary started to Stalk. She saw how her mother and father had both been from abusive environments, and how they had recreated those environments with her. Her mother had been emotionally and sexually abused. Her father had been sexually and physically abused. Mary Stalked herself, her life, her patterns, and her wounds. She began to heal her wounds by falling in love with them rather than judging them. She took one step at a time and was very gentle with herself. Gradually, she started to have more awareness. She began to change her pattern of craving attention, love, and gentleness from others. Little by little she became more content in life. She made the choice to change some bad situations, including getting a divorce. In doing so, she protected both herself and her daughter and began to transform the pattern of abuse.

Mary was finally loving herself and treating herself with respect and gentleness. Therefore, her craving for love and respect from others stopped. She put a higher price on herself; she wouldn't date just anyone to be in a relationship. She only dated men who treated her very well, and with the greatest respect. She felt okay being alone, too, because she no longer needed the approval of others to feel all right about herself. She saw herself as a better person and liked herself. Mary was really enjoying her life.

If you are part of a cycle of abusive behavior, it continues in your life because of the energy and the wounds that you carry. You are attracted to others with the same energy field. The same mirror, or reflection, returns to you again and again. The only way you can shift it and break the cycle, or pattern, is by going into your wounds and healing them. Your wounds and your unhappiness run deep. You can put on a great mask and say you're content, that your relationship is growing and that you're working things out. But you can only work out so much with someone else when you can't work things out inside yourself. The healing really begins with you.

9

THE STAR OF FREEDOM

The Dream

IN THE DREAM OF THE PLANET, YOU COMMUNICATE
through words. If you wanted to express what freedom is,
you would probably first try to describe it in words. You
would most likely be able to describe aspects of it, but you
would have trouble expressing the essence of it. The same
thing happens when you see a cloud and try to describe it.
One moment it looks like a beautiful angel and the next
moment like a monster. Every moment that cloud transforms
into a new form, a new energy. You can't truly describe the
essence of the cloud, but you can describe what it looks like
to you at a particular moment. And different people see different things in the cloud. You might see the cloud as a house,

while another person might say it looks like a dragon. But it is still a cloud. The same is true of your perception of freedom. One moment you might describe freedom a particular way, but the next moment something happens to you and your perception of freedom changes. And freedom may look different to you than to the next person, but you both use the word *freedom* to describe your perceptions.

Your perception of freedom is very tied to the belief system within which you live. If you live in America, the "land of the free," your belief system tells you that you are free compared to people in other countries. Your Constitution tells you all the ways you are free, and you live the American Dream and see life through that domestication. However, you still have to pay taxes and worry about meeting your bills. There are also a lot of rules to follow, and if you don't do so, there are consequences. You may even go to jail. These types of things may take away your happiness, so you are not truly free. Your feelings or perceptions of freedom exist within the rules and structure of the system. As an American, however, you may be more free than someone from another country with a different government and different rules. In some countries you cannot speak out against the government without risking your life. In America you can complain about the government all the time, and the freedom to do so is a right.

The wounds that you carry also affect your perception of freedom. For example, you may think you are free if you jump from one brief relationship to another and never commit to a single person or get "tied down." You justify your actions by saying you just want to have fun. However, it is usually your wounds that keep you from going deeper into a relationship. Jumping from one person to another is easier than working through any problems that come up with a particular partner. It also keeps you from looking at your inner self and your wounds, which are always reflected in the mirror of your partner. Running away also prevents your partner from seeing through the masks you put on to hook your partner in the early stages of dating.

When you master the war inside your mind and heart through discipline and awareness, you heal your wounds, and you are no longer affected by the belief system. You finally see what freedom truly is. It is freedom of the spirit. No matter what your situation may be, nothing can take your happiness and contentment away from you. The experience of true freedom was perhaps something you never tasted or understood before. Maybe you always understood it through your domestication, even if it was what you said you always wanted in life.

Before I became a warrior, I had no idea what freedom was. It did not relate to my life. Freedom only existed as a word. The only thing that I thought was free was a bird. Maybe that was why I used to ride horses wildly and drive my motorcycle fast. The wind rushing through my hair made me feel as if I was flying like a bird—like I was free. Although I was not aware of it earlier in my life, I was always searching for freedom. That was why I did a lot of drinking and drugs—they were the closest experiences I could get to freedom at the time. Later, as a warrior, when I became truly free, I realized that freedom was not about wind or speed or being uninhibited on drugs. I learned that I was in flight like a bird every moment. And I didn't even have to move. My spirit was free. Once I realized this in my being, I became the Star of Freedom. In every moment I was content and enjoyed life to the fullest.

Words of the Star of Freedom

Visualize the word *freedom* as a bright ray of light in the center of a star. It is the divine connection with pure love. There are other words created out of that center, such as *happiness, enjoyment, contentment, peacefulness,* and *playfulness.* All of these words have different rays of light, yet all are part of the ray of light that is freedom. These words and their rays of light get blocked by the emotional wounds you carry, which come from your life experiences. For example, perhaps you are serious instead of being playful because when you were a child your father left and never came home, abandoning you and your family. So at an early age you were forced to be an adult, getting a job to help the family. This wound now creates a block that prevents you from feeling the ray of light that is playful. However, as you do work on the Toltec path and remove the block, you may one day start to feel playful.

Experiencing each word, or ray of light, is not necessarily an all-or-nothing process. There are different levels of each word. The level you experience depends upon the wounds you carry. You may always be serious but sometimes feel content. As you continue to work on the path, you may reach different levels of experiencing each word, and you may eventually touch all the words. You may move from always being serious to sometimes being playful. To do so, you remove some of the blockage, heal the wound, and touch the word that is playful. Then you start to see, feel, and live life in different ways. And since all these words lead back into the ray of light that is freedom, at each level of your growth you get another taste of freedom and its connection to divine love.

When you begin to work on yourself, you start at the outermost reaches of the rays of light. Over time, as you reach different levels, you move toward the center of the star, toward freedom. In this process you become the words through working on yourself. You become happiness, contentment, and so on. This only occurs through transformation: through seeing all feelings as yourself, and embracing them. Once you start to transform the badness or sadness, and fall in love with the anger and pain as they manifest inside you, you start feeling the different levels of freedom and its rays.

Where you are now in life—the extent to which you experience each of these words—depends upon your ray of light and its unique vibration inside your physical being. Each person in the Dream, as well as each bird, each tree, and each thing that exists, has its own personal ray of light that is always connected to the Source, to God, to the Creator. And that ray of light is how much energy and information you get from the Source. Some people are born into life with a ray of light that is more expanded because of the work they have done in past lives. But no matter how much energy you start off with in life, the more work you do the more your ray of light expands, and the more you experience the different levels of each word. As you work, you feel more and more happiness and contentment. The intent is to eventually expand your ray of light to the point that it has no limitations. You become everything, and the words aren't important anymore.

Awareness is the key to expanding your ray of light and moving toward freedom. It is the awareness of yourself, of your every action, and of how you see life. Awareness allows you to see patterns so that you can make choices. You can decide whether or not to stay in a relationship when an old, unhealthy pattern emerges, and whether to question a belief system. Your level of awareness allows you to know that there is something else in life besides that which is presented by the Dream of the Planet. And it is the Mastery of Awareness that helps you search for and find your own personal truth and become the Star of Freedom.

10

THE ELEVEN AGREEMENTS OF THE SPIRITUAL WARRIOR

Taking Action

THIS CHAPTER IS ABOUT TAKING ACTION. PREVIOUS chapters have described your wounds and the ways that you may be unhappy. This chapter focuses on what to do about your wounds. There are a number of guidelines that you must follow if you wish to be on the path of the Spiritual Warrior. In fact, they are more than just guidelines. They are the new spiritual agreements you must make with yourself in order to create a life in which your spirit can be free. They describe what you must do in order to break the agreements of the Dream of the Planet that imprison your soul.

There are eleven agreements for you to follow as a Spiritual Warrior. They are:

1. Awareness
2. Discipline
3. Nonjudgment
4. Respect
5. Patience
6. Trust
7. Love
8. Impeccability of Environment
9. Honesty
10. Taking Action
11. Impeccability of Energy

These spiritual agreements form a pyramid; they are guides along your path. The foundation of this pyramid, and the foundation of all of the other agreements, is awareness. Awareness is also the tip of the pyramid—the result of all the work you do on the path of the Toltec warrior. In fact, the work of the Toltec warrior is the Mastery of Awareness.

1. Awareness

Mastering awareness means becoming aware of everything about yourself. It means being aware of your personal life and of how you see yourself, feel about yourself, think about yourself, and speak about yourself. It means no longer seeing the faults of or judging others. You know inside your heart that pointing your finger and blaming others has truly not worked—that your unhappiness is within you. Mastering awareness is the key to changing the patterns of emotion and behavior that make you unhappy. The starting point is having the awareness that you truly want to change—for *yourself*. The work of increasing your awareness then involves being aware of what you are doing every moment of your life, and being aware of your breath, which is your energy exchange with the universe.

Once you decide that you truly want to change and you begin to do work, you need to practice being 100 percent present in the moment and totally focused on what you are doing while simultaneously being aware of your breath. This takes a lot of effort. It is difficult at first to learn to be in the moment because your mind is constantly thinking. You may be planning something or making arrangements for something, even as simple as lunch. In conversation you may be thinking about what you are going to say next, or about what you feel you should be doing instead of talking. There is constant chatter that goes on in your mind, much of which you are probably not even aware of since it is habit. So how do you stop your mind's chatter in order to focus on being in the moment?

Exercise: Your assignment for the next twelve hours of being awake is to focus on what you are thinking at all times. Keep a journal of how many times during any particular activity thoughts about other things pop into your mind. For example, if you are talking on the phone with your mother, be aware of intrusive thoughts. When you get off the phone, write down how many times during the conversation you were thinking about something else, such as what you were going to make for dinner. If you are driving, be aware of how many different directions your mind goes in. When you get to where you are going, write down all the things you were thinking about instead of concentrating on driving.

Exercise: Be aware of your breathing at all times. Focus first on your in-breath, then on your out-breath, then on your in-breath, then on your out-breath during all activities, and at all times during the day. When you realize that you have lost your focus, shift your attention back to your breathing. This is an ongoing exercise that is the key to awareness in every moment. Therefore it is important to do it frequently and throughout your work as a Spiritual Warrior.

Focusing on your breathing does not mean that you need to sit and be still all day long. In fact, this practice involves actively living life as a human being and creating your existence while focusing and being present in the moment. If you are an artist who has a deadline for a painting, you would be present as you paint while simultaneously being focused on your breath. Nothing else would exist in those moments other than the painting and your breath, which is your life. When the telephone rings you would pick up the phone and focus only on the conversation, nothing else. You would be 100 percent present with the person on the telephone. There would be no thoughts of painting, or deadlines. You would be opening your awareness to living life in each moment.

What does living life in each moment mean? It means that you live life with the Angel of Life and you live life with the Angel of Death with every breath you take. You only have this present moment in life; you never really know if there will be a next one. So living each moment fully gives you the chance to have no regrets that you missed out on things. There are ways you might experience many regrets in life. You might say, "I wish I had told my mother I loved her before she died." Or suddenly you become ill or disabled and you can't do something you had always wanted to because you put it off until tomorrow. Or you are a new mother who is so preoccupied with cleaning house and cooking dinner that you miss the joy of hearing your child's first word or seeing his first step.

Living life in the moment expands your level of awareness and your perception of life. After practicing it for a while, you can perceive a great deal around you without it distracting you. This practice keeps you focused on what you are doing while maintaining your awareness on what else is happening. An eagle has awareness of every little feather that creates its flight, but this doesn't distract the eagle from the actual flight.

Eduardo, the man who wanted the promotion, was thinking so much about how the day was going to be that he wasn't living in the moment. All of his awareness was on the promotion. As he was having his breakfast and coffee and his wife was talking to him, he was thinking, "Who's getting the promotion? Am I getting the promotion or is the other guy getting the promotion? What will I say and how will I act if I don't get the promotion? How will I act if I do get the promotion? What will I be like if I get the promotion?" Eduardo wasn't concentrating on having breakfast with his family. He wasn't even aware that his wife was talking to him, and he wasn't aware that this might be the last moment he would see his children. Eduardo could have walked out the door after breakfast and been hit by a car. He was not living life fully in the moment, and he was not aware of the presence of his gifts.

2. Discipline

Awareness helps you to create discipline, which is the second agreement of the Spiritual Warrior. When you have enough awareness to realize that this path is what you want to do, then discipline is the process that helps you follow through with this choice. Discipline allows you to respect your word so much that you will follow through on the action associated with your word. Whatever you say you are going to do, you complete your word one step at a time with discipline. Discipline is very important for all levels of the Spiritual Warrior, but especially the beginning Spiritual Warrior.

As a beginning Spiritual Warrior, you might make too many promises or set too many goals for yourself. As a result, you might not be fully focused on each goal and so you might not follow through on it. Discipline helps you start one goal and complete it. It assists you in being 100 percent focused and giving it all you've got. After, you will master discipline enough that you will be able to do two things simultaneously and give each of them 100 percent of your awareness.

As a beginning Spiritual Warrior who makes a commitment to look at yourself, you need a lot of discipline to stick with the process. After a while, you may start to feel tired of working a certain way, or you may not want to look at a certain wound. It is easier to walk away than to follow through on your word of commitment. It takes a lot of discipline to choose to break old patterns.

Discipline is really about making a choice to take action, to go forward 100 percent. No matter what is presented, discipline gives you the willpower to overcome any boulders that are in your path. Discipline guides you to embrace the boulders for a while and then to walk over them. Discipline is about respecting your word, knowing you are connected to the Source, and realizing that you can embrace, overcome, and heal any wound.

3. Nonjudgment

The third spiritual agreement is nonjudgment. Once you choose to be a Spiritual Warrior, from that moment on you must not judge yourself, or anyone or anything else. It is time to forgive yourself. Judgment is the biggest thing that keeps you from looking at yourself. When you are judging yourself, you are also pointing your finger at other people and saying, "Look at them and what they are doing!" The intent of nonjudgment is to have enough awareness that you know when you are starting to judge someone else or yourself. You know when you are being too hard on yourself. You know when your expectations of yourself are too high, and you are setting yourself up for self-judgment when your expectations aren't fulfilled. As you become aware of judgment, the intent is to shift yourself into non-judgment using your breath, your awareness of the moment, and the flow of the breath of life.

4. Respect

The fourth spiritual agreement is respect. It is most important to accept and respect yourself 100 percent the way you are: to view all aspects of yourself as perfect, including your body, your words, your thoughts, and your actions. It is also important that you have great respect for everyone and everything else.

Respect is a challenge for the beginning Spiritual Warrior. If you don't know how to respect yourself, it may be impossible to respect others. Initially, your awareness of how you are thinking about yourself may come with various forms of judgment. For example, you may not like your body's weight or the fact that you are shy.

Those kinds of judgment mean you are not accepting and respecting yourself 100 percent. They also mean that you cannot fully respect other people who are overweight or shy: you judge them too.

Eduardo is a good example of someone who didn't respect himself. He had discipline in the sense that he worked hard in the world to be educated and move ahead in life; however, he also had the agreement that the other culture was better and that he had to work extra hard to prove himself. It would have been extremely difficult for Eduardo (or anyone else) to have overcome this agreement, because such agreements are based on fear, and anything that is based on fear is not based on respect. Eduardo was afraid he wasn't good enough and that he might be a "failure." He judged himself very harshly, and therefore he did not respect himself. He was also not living life in the moment.

When you are hard on yourself, not living life in the moment, and thinking about something else, you are not respecting yourself and you are not respecting the people you are with. You are also not respecting the gift of life in that moment.

Achieving respect takes all three of the other agreements discussed so far. It takes awareness of the moment, disciplining yourself to reach one goal at a time, and nonjudgment. These three agreements give you more energy to embrace yourself. You feel more complete when you are in the moment and you have the discipline to complete one goal with truth. You respect yourself more, feel more content and joyous, and live even more in the moment. Then you know that you are connected to the Source, which created everything in life. It is also much clearer to you that you are special, which in turn creates an even greater respect for yourself and for life. This process keeps building until you respect yourself every moment in every breath.

5. Patience

The fifth spiritual agreement is patience. It is healing to be gentle, kind, and most of all patient with yourself. Being patient is the greatest gift you can give yourself. It is also very challenging because you, like most people, probably want things to happen overnight. You are used to getting things done and feeling an immediate sense of accomplishment. However, spiritual transformation is a process that takes time. You are giving yourself a great gift if you allow yourself to patiently go into the process of looking at your wounds. To do so, open the door to your wounds fully. Look at your wounds, embrace them, and then clean them out gradually and patiently. Fill your wounds with every vibration of love. To support your patience, stay in the moment, feel the pain, and know that with every breath things are shifting and healing whether you see the process or not. Healing yourself patiently is treating yourself with the greatest respect and love, and giving yourself the most special gift.

6. Trust

Trust is the sixth agreement of the Spiritual Warrior. Trust is a powerful word. You may have never had the opportunity to truly trust yourself. Your upbringing taught you certain rules that defined your experience of trust. You learned that if you followed these rules, you had "trust." For example, perhaps you learned that you can trust your partner if he or she follows the rules of not flirting or dating others, and of being devoted to you in action. You are considered trustworthy if you do the same. Or perhaps, if you are the manager of a supermarket, you trust the cashiers if they follow the rules of not stealing and of accurately ringing up orders.

Trust for the Spiritual Warrior is different; it is about being fully present for yourself. You are the bird choosing to fly out of the nest. As a Spiritual Warrior, you choose to become an apprentice to yourself, to Spirit, and to the whole universe. You choose to become the Jaguar

Knight taking your first flight into trust. This form of trust may be unknown to you at the beginning; it may not be familiar because it is not about rules. It is about trusting your inner voice, the true self within you. And sometimes trusting your inner voice may be breaking the rules, and that can be scary. Trust is about knowing that you will be guided in your journey, and that you have to surrender and let go.

7. Love

Love is the seventh agreement of the Spiritual Warrior. To follow this agreement, you must love yourself as you love the gurus, the saints, Jesus, or Allah. Love is inside you and not separate from you. Love is you, so you always need to love yourself with compassion.

As a beginning apprentice, a Jaguar Knight, you experience these words of agreement as a certain vibration, based on where you are in your own growth process. For example, your understanding of love may be based on what you have experienced in relationships, perhaps a love based on need and dependency. That is not the truest form of love. As you continue to work on the path, you may experience these words of agreement as a different vibration, based on how your understanding of love changes. Before you can truly love someone else, you have to love yourself, and to do so means you have to look inside yourself at your wounds and patterns. You must respect yourself enough to open the door, trust yourself enough to take the first step, and have patience with your process. Love will transform every moment that you choose to embrace yourself and your wounds.

When you work spiritually, you develop a certain deep love for yourself. You may then be drawn to teachers who have reached the goal of reflecting the highest form of love. These teachers and gurus are great mirrors for reflecting love and for helping you to transform love and reflect it to others. However, always look at yourself in the mirror and know that you yourself are the teachers and gurus; you are not separate from any of them.

8. Impeccability of Environment

The eighth spiritual agreement is to surround yourself with an impeccable environment. The environment you create is very important because it is a reflection of you. When you start to clean your internal self, to look inside your heart and open internal doors and wounds, you especially need to create an external environment that is clean and that reflects the guru inside yourself. Practically speaking, this means you need to pick up any messes and clean your home. Your home is your temple. So add some touches to brighten your living space or make it more homelike. Focus also on your own appearance. Keep your clothes clean, ironed, and neat. You are cleaning up your outside self in the same way you are cleaning up your inside self.

9. Honesty

There are three parts to the ninth spiritual agreement. The first part is to be honest with yourself: to look into your heart and decide what you really want, and how you really feel. The second part is to speak your truth. This follows being honest with yourself. Once you look into your heart and honestly know your truth, then you can speak your truth. Tell people what you think and feel. No more lies and no more hiding. The third part of this agreement is a rule for action, based on the first two parts: Don't go against yourself. Don't do anything that goes against your heart or your spirit.

Your whole intent in becoming a Spiritual Warrior is to learn to speak your truth and to follow that little voice that guides you every moment. That little voice and your truth become stronger as you transform to be more honest with yourself and to listen to your heart.

The only way not to go against yourself is to feel your truth: to look into your heart and know that you no longer want to continue a certain pattern. You make a choice. That pattern is something you've already done, a taste you've already had that you don't want in your life anymore. Remembering the pain or other emotions you felt when you were in that pattern will encourage you not to go against yourself when the pattern comes up again.

All of the spiritual agreements build upon each other. In order not to go against yourself, you need to develop awareness of your patterns. Once an agreement is given to you, a pattern of behavior is created. Then it becomes automatic for you to continue that pattern of behavior. It is what you know; it is familiar. Perhaps as a child you were given the agreement that children should be seen and not heard. You took on this agreement and then carried it through your life as an automatic way of being. Even though now as an adult person you may want to say how you feel or what you think, you automatically remain quiet because that agreement makes you feel you have nothing worthwhile to say. In remaining quiet, you are going against how you really feel, which is wanting to express yourself. So the challenge is to have enough awareness and courage to transform this automatic behavior.

As you start to do work as a Spiritual Warrior and a Jaguar Knight, you begin to have more awareness. Eventually, as you stay more present in the moment, reclaim your energy, and take responsibility for your actions, your level of energy increases. In turn, that increased energy helps you transform each pattern. So your intent as a Spiritual Warrior is to not go against yourself, to be honest, and to speak your truth as clearly as possible in every moment.

As an example, perhaps your lifestyle in the past included a lot of partying. The people you hung out with were always doing drugs and drinking alcohol, and that was how you socialized with them. They were your really good friends in life. But you knew that you were truly miserable, so one day you decided you wanted to get out of that dream. That lifestyle was not working for you anymore. You became sick and lost your job; you were not content in life. You decided that you wanted to create a new environment for yourself in which you respected your body and treated yourself in a way you had never done before. So you looked at yourself honestly. With this increased awareness, you decided what you wanted to change or let go of in your life, and what you wanted to keep. Because of this honesty with yourself, each step in your process of change was about not going against yourself. You honored the self of truth that wanted to transform.

However, in leaving that life behind, you missed your former friends, and still sometimes wanted to be around them. The greatest tests occurred when you were invited to that old environment. It felt so familiar; it was something you knew so well. Automatically a part of you wanted to fall right back into your old lifestyle because it was safe, it was home, and it was something you had done for years. And your Parasite was telling you, "Oh, who cares, you know this is really what you want to do. You really want to go smoke some pot and drink some beer." But the part of you that was transforming looked at your truth: that you did not want to do drugs. So you made the choice not to do drugs—not to do that to your body anymore. You went into that environment and did not go against yourself. This was a result of being strong and truthful with yourself.

When your friends came up to you and suggested that you smoke some pot, or snort a line of cocaine, or have a beer, you were able to speak your truth. Deep down inside you felt strongly committed to your decision, so you told them, "No, I really made a choice to quit and that's what I'm doing. I'm choosing to be here with you because I enjoy your company, but that doesn't mean I have to do what you're doing to have a good time."

Eventually you and your partying friends grew apart because you had nothing in common but old memories. You stopped associating with them, not because you judged them or didn't like them, but because you were transforming. You started to meet people who were also transforming, and in spending time with them you created a new environment for yourself. These new people became close, like family. You trusted yourself and moved away from the past with love and respect.

10. Taking Action

Every moment there are things to manifest or transform in your life. But for the transformation to occur, you have to take action. This is the tenth spiritual agreement. You can dream about changing your life but that doesn't mean you are going to do it. It is your responsibility not only to look into your heart and see your patterns every day, but to take action to make changes in your life. You can do so with the assistance of the other spiritual agreements.

11. Impeccability of Energy

The eleventh and final spiritual agreement is impeccability of energy. When you make the choice to become a Jaguar Knight and you begin to take action in your life, you are claiming energy and personal power for yourself. Personal power arises from how you place your energy every moment in your life: during your conversations with people, during your silence with yourself, during your work activities. In every activity, personal power arises from how you place your energy. Being impeccable with your energy means being aware every moment of your energy field and how you are using it as your personal power. When you use your energy with impeccability, you have reverence for all life and for the mirror of yourself in everything around you. You have the greatest respect for yourself and the power of your words in communication with others. For example, not engaging in gossip is an impeccable use of energy. An unimpeccable use of energy would be to send out sexual energy in all your interactions because deep down your wounds make you crave attention, even though you don't really like yourself and are not close to loving and respecting yourself. The more Stalking you do, the more awareness you have, and the more impeccable you become with your energy.

Mary, who came from an abusive family, was miserable in her marriage and wanted to get out of it. She and her husband were never really honest with each other; they were just living a pattern, a routine. Marriage gave them a sense of security because it was a known, familiar structure that they had built around themselves. It was a pattern that provided protection from the outside world. They were afraid to break through the barriers they had created. But there really were no barriers; Mary could have walked away whenever she wanted. The only barriers that existed were in her mind.

Mary became so desperate living within the barriers she had created that she finally made the choice to change her life. She became an apprentice to herself, to the universe, and to God to work toward becoming a Jaguar Knight. She Stalked all the events that she had experienced as a little girl. She visualized that she was special, that the abuse had not been her fault, that she had had no choice at that time since she had been a child, and that she could now forgive herself. In that forgiveness, she saw that she now had a choice because she was not a little girl anymore. She could choose to stay in her current relationship, which was an unhappy, abusive situation, or move on. Mary looked into her heart and was honest with herself. She saw that she did not love her husband. Mary also saw the pattern of relationships in her life: the cycle of abuse with herself and her daughter and the fear of being alone. With great courage she made the choice to break the pattern and move on, even if it meant being alone, which was one of her greatest fears.

She wanted to take care of herself and her child and to heal herself fully. The respect Mary had for herself was growing, and she was able to speak her truth to her husband. Her truth was that she wanted to leave. Mary was not going to go against herself anymore. She was going to leave the marriage.

Mary's words and actions were impeccable. The impeccability came from respecting herself highly and from raising her price in life. She loved herself and saw herself as very special. She chose to look into her heart, to see her truth, to speak it honestly to her husband, and not to go against herself no matter what it took and how much fear she had to face. She moved on.

11

STALKING

Shifting the Dream

THE PROCESS OF TRANSFORMATION BEGINS WITH THE search for a new way of looking at life. You start this search when you become aware that your life isn't working anymore and you are not content with every breath. A similar awareness has brought you to read this book. On the Toltec path, the first action you take as a seeker is to find a *nagual*, the highest teacher on this path. Naguals have achieved mastery at all levels of this work. In reading this book, you are taking the first step; you are searching for something better in life, and you have found the teachings of a nagual.

The second step on the Toltec path is to become a Toltec warrior, an apprentice. Becoming an apprentice means making a commitment to learn and then following through on the process, even if it is difficult to look within yourself at times. In the past, the Toltec path involved becoming an apprentice to a person who was a nagual, but only a select group of people had this opportunity. Today the dream of the warrior exists in a different way. Instead of becoming an apprentice to a nagual, you become an apprentice to yourself with guidance from the teachings of a nagual. The lessons in this book are such teachings. They are available to anyone who is interested. Although the work is now open to everyone, becoming an apprentice is still a serious commitment. You are giving your word to yourself that you will do your best and work 100 percent toward self-transformation.

There are two levels on the Toltec path that you pass through in the course of your quest for transformation. The first level of Toltec warrior is the Jaguar Knight, and the second level is the Eagle Knight. Moving through these levels is a process of opening the doors of your heart. The key to unlocking these doors is becoming the jaguar. This begins when you enter the first level of work and become a Jaguar Knight.

The Level of the Jaguar Knight

The Toltecs called the first level of apprenticeship the Jaguar Knight because of the importance they placed on the jaguar and its ways. They felt that the jaguar was a great teacher for those who were willing to learn from it, because they saw it as a master stalker, living and hunting on the earth. They perceived the jaguar as alert, still, and focused totally in the moment. So at the first level of work, the Toltecs visualized themselves as the jaguar, the great stalker, in order to become the greatest Stalkers of themselves.

Stalking is a strong word in the Dream of the Planet. It may bring up fearful images for you of one person stalking another. But the Toltec form of Stalking is not about Stalking other people. It is about Stalking yourself. As a Toltec warrior, you look within yourself.

When you take the step to become a Spiritual Warrior, you visualize yourself with cat eyes through which you look at yourself every moment in life. You hunt everything you experience as a human being on this earth: the patterns of how you live your life, how you gossip, how you think about and judge others, how you talk about and judge yourself, how you act, and what you feel. You are not deciding whether things are good or bad, positive or negative. You are not judging yourself as bad because you are gossiping. No, of course not. You are re-claiming the energy you have lost in exchanges, connect-ing with your truth, and healing.

You look into your heart and see where the sadness, anger, and discontent are, opening the doors closed by these wounds. Like many people, your doors may be sealed with nicely painted locks that say you've already dealt with these feelings, or that they existed in the past and are therefore not now important. The intent is to feel safe enough to look at these parts of you that are blocked behind the doors in order to heal and become the full being that you are.

The jaguar heals its wounds by licking and loving them. When you look within yourself, you open your wounds with patience and love. You embrace the sad-ness and hurt in your heart, without blame. Healing is not about blaming others or yourself. Pointing your fin-ger and blaming someone does nothing to change situa-tions or make you happy. It does not change patterns or heal the wounds causing them. The wounds themselves are the source of your unhappiness. Healing is about ac-cepting full responsibility for your life. It is about taking action to change the patterns and heal the wounds.

Stalking is taking action. It is a tool given to you by a

nagual that helps you look at the agreements given to you by the Dream of the Planet and then clean your wounds and transform your patterns. Stalking also helps you take responsibility for the energy you have directed at others through agreements you have given and through harsh words you have spoken. Other people are not responsible for the words you give them every day. You are. Stalking uses the power of the breath to heal. The power of the breath is love and respect. Healing is always done with the greatest love and respect for yourself.

As you heal the wounds and let go of the sadness, you reclaim all of the energy you have used in interactions with others and have left floating around throughout your life. This strengthens your willpower, and you develop the awareness to break patterns and realize that the things you do in life are your choice. Then you can make positive choices for yourself and, when you encounter problems, your reactions are no longer so extreme or emotionally consuming. Instead, you are able to shift your focus to release the impact of the problems. You are detached enough that problems no longer take your happiness. You are able to live life more in the moment. You start to feel happy and content, and to live life to the fullest. This process takes time. When you are at the level of the Jaguar Knight, you are still fighting a battle with the Parasite and the deep wounds that are inside yourself. When you reach the point that you feel happy and content most of the time, then you have become the jaguar. You have mastered its lessons. You then enter the next level of the Toltec work: the Eagle Knight.

The Level of the Eagle Knight

For Toltec warriors, the level beyond the Jaguar Knight is the Eagle Knight. The eagle is also viewed as a great teacher. As an apprentice, once you master the lessons of the jaguar, you focus on mastering the lessons of the eagle. Becoming an Eagle Knight means shifting from walking on earth as a jaguar to flying in the sky as an eagle. The eagle soars. Visualize looking through its eyes and experiencing its perceptions. In flight it looks down on the earth, which is a very different view from that of the jaguar on earth. Whereas the jaguar focuses in on the object of its hunt, the eagle perceives two realities in every moment: the reality of the hunt (like the jaguar), and the reality of the surrounding environment. The eagle's perception of the hunt and what it is going to eat comes from the jaguar inside it. The jaguar is the zoom lens that picks a point to focus on. The eagle is the lens that sees the broader environment, the expanded vision around its prey.

When you become an Eagle Knight, you do not look at life from a single perspective anymore. You develop a tremendous amount of awareness, including the awareness of having balance. Your human side is still connected to the earth, fully living life each moment. Yet you also take flight and expand your awareness out toward God, or the Source. The eagle is your spirit. You experience the Source and know what it feels like, even though you may be unable to hold on to that feeling every moment. You also have enough awareness that you feel contentment, which is a great gift. So as an Eagle Knight you live in both the dream of heaven and the dream of earth.

As an Eagle Knight you experience the ray of light that is freedom, the center of the star discussed in chapter 9. From that freedom radiates contentment, happiness, and joy. You are more playful. As an Eagle Knight you feel this way more often than you do as a Jaguar Knight, but this doesn't mean that the other emotions such as sadness, guilt, shame, and so on are gone entirely for you. These emotions may still be there, but you have a tremendous amount of awareness, so you can shift them much more quickly. You don't fall into the emotions; you are not a victim anymore. You don't allow your Parasite to feed the emotions with thoughts such as, "Why me? Why are they treating me that way?" or with feeling sorry for yourself. As an Eagle Knight you are aware that you are feeling the emotions, but you keep your focus on everything that is happening in the moment. You feel what you feel and then you let it go.

Not everybody becomes an Eagle Knight, but once you do, your own flight, which is your personal and spiritual growth, continues. Your growth is endless. When you master this level, you become heaven on earth. You may even go on to claim your power as a nagual, the highest level on the Toltec path. This, however, is rare.

The Journey Begins

Now that you are ready to heal and transform, take a few moments to make the commitment and become an apprentice to yourself. This is an act of love, a gift you are giving to yourself. Following are a ceremony and prayer to assist you in becoming a Jaguar Knight.

To become an apprentice to yourself, light a candle and sit in a quiet place. Clear your mind. Sit up straight and look into the flame as you clearly speak these words of power:

I, your name, choose to love and respect myself in this new beginning of my life. I will be present with myself and as honest as I can. I will open the door to trust myself at a new level, and to forgive myself and others. I will learn to love my breath every moment. I love ME.

Now it is time to learn the art of Stalking yourself. You are the jaguar. There are two parts to Stalking: the technique and the practice.

The Technique of Stalking

The act of breathing is powerful; it is a life-giving, cleansing process on a physical level. With each in-breath you take in oxygen, a life-giving force, and with each out-breath you give back carbon dioxide, a substance that your body has no use for. With Stalking, the same cleansing process occurs on an energetic level. When you use the power of your breath to Stalk, you exchange energy with both aspects of your breathing, your in-breath and your out-breath.

The in-breath. The in-breath is used when you want to reclaim something you gave to someone else or yourself, such as harsh words or a judgment. You hold the image of whatever interaction or situation you are reviewing in your mind's eye. As you breathe in (take an in-breath), you visualize whatever it is you want to come back to you, and you see it filtering through your body down into Mother Earth. Mother Earth is nonjudgmental and will embrace the energy you filter into her. For any given image, you may want to use the in-breath several times. Wait until you feel in your heart that the energy exchange is complete. When you are focusing on the in-breath, the out-breath just helps you maintain your breathing rhythm; there is no need to focus your attention on it.

The out-breath. The out-breath is used when you want to give something back to someone. This is something they gave to you that doesn't belong to you. It can be any strong emotion such as anger, hatred, or resentment that was directed at you, or any seeds or words of strong intent. For example, if someone tells you that you are stupid, that word has a very strong intent; it is a seed. A seed is a powerful agreement that affects what you believe about yourself after it is given to you.

During Stalking, hold the image of whatever interaction or situation you are reviewing in your mind's eye. Using the out-breath, give back the emotion, agreement, or seed. Perform the out-breath with a forceful blow: picture yourself blowing a mosquito off your arm. For any given image, you may want to use the out-breath several times. Wait until you feel in your heart that the energy exchange is complete. When you are focusing on the out-breath, the in-breath just helps you maintain your breathing rhythm; there is no need to focus your attention on it.

For some images you may just use the in-breath to take things back. Do this one or more times for each image. For other images you may just use the out-breath to give things back. And yet other times you may use both the in- and out-breath. Always breathe until you feel complete, and trust yourself. The specific images and areas to focus on depend upon the level of Stalking. The levels of Stalking are described in the next section.

You may feel uncomfortable giving back energy forms such as agreements and harsh words to the people who gave them to you. You might think you could just give them back to the earth, or to energy. It is true that everything in life is energy, and everything carries its own personal vibration. A plant carries a certain vibration, and the ground it is on carries a different one. But during the cycle of your soul as a human being, you are responsible for every action you take in life. When you take back energy forms such as agreements and harsh words that belong to you, you complete your destiny and the cycle of your soul. When you return the energy given to you by others, it helps these people complete their destinies and the cycles of their souls.

When you are breathing your intent and giving back agreements, always do so with love. And when you reclaim energy, do so with the intent of love. Every breath is pure love; it is the essence of life. Have this awareness be automatic; it is not something you need to focus on or speak about.

The Practice of Stalking

Sessions in which you are going to Stalk should last at least one hour, and should be done daily. Any time of day is fine, but the best time is when you are undisturbed for the full hour. It is good if no one else is around, your phone is picked up by the answering machine, and your pager is turned off. Most sessions consist of four parts. The first part is a meditation for opening and cleansing your heart, which is a preparation for Stalking. The second part is the Stalking itself, with the focus dependent upon the level of Stalking. The third part is reflection, a time to share your experiences if you are working with a group or to write in a journal or speak into a recorder if you are working alone. Writing in a journal helps you see what issues are coming up for you and allows you to reflect on your patterns of behavior. Down the road it also shows you how far you have come. If you are working in a group, it is also good to use a journal after you share your experiences. However, if time constraints are an issue, then using a journal is optional. The fourth part of the session is a closing, healing meditation.

There are five levels of Stalking. They should be done in order and for the time period indicated. Each level should be completed before you start on the next one. The first three levels are considered to be stages of the Jaguar Knight. The fourth and fifth levels are stages of the Eagle Knight.

Descriptions of the five levels of Stalking follow. Each description contains all the information you need to work at that level. Therefore, some of the information is repeated in order for each section to be a practical, working guide. However, much of the information changes from level to level, so read each description carefully before you begin working at that level.

LEVEL 1 STALKING: STAR FORMATION

Items needed:
quartz crystal that fits in the palm of your hand
pillow for your head
rug or blanket to lie on
journal or tape recorder

1. Heart Meditation. The Heart Meditation opens your heart in preparation for Stalking.

Lie on your back on the floor inside your house, or outside on the ground. Place your palms flat, facing down. For comfort, you can use a pillow for your head

and lie on a blanket or rug. Close your eyes. Take some
deep breaths and focus on relaxing yourself. Feel your
body lying on the ground and totally surrender yourself
to Mother Earth. Let go of any physical tension you are
holding, and any thoughts in your mind. Focus on the
rhythm of your breath.

After a few moments, visualize a small version of
yourself at this moment in your life. See this small version of you entering your mouth and then walking
through your mouth and down your throat toward your
heart. As you get near your heart, visualize a door. Since
you are creating this door, it can appear any way you
want. It can be made of the most beautiful gold, or be
intricately carved out of wood, or just be very simple.
Whatever works for you. Then open the door and enter
your heart. Look inside your heart with honest eyes.
What do you see? Who are the people you love that you
carry inside your heart? This is the time to let them go
free. The people you love do not belong to you; love is
not controlling. This moment is about releasing the images you have created of these people out of love. Let
their spirits fly. To do so, first thank them for being there
in your heart. Then, as you breathe out, release them one
at a time. Continue breathing out and releasing them
until you feel complete. When you are done, visualize a

beautiful ray of light from the sun inside your heart. This ray of light is pure love, and it will nourish and stay with you always. After a few moments, open your eyes.

The intent of this meditation is to clean your heart, the purest temple that ever existed, and to fill it with pure love. The little version of you that enters your heart the first time you do this meditation will continue to live there. Because of this, you will love yourself more and more unconditionally each time you complete the meditation. You will also respect yourself as you would the highest queen, king, guru, or other image of purity. That image of purity is you.

2. Stalking. After completing the Heart Meditation, continue to lie down with your palms flat on Mother Earth, which is the floor inside your house or the ground outside. You can also continue to use a pillow for your head and a blanket to lie on. If you are working with a group, have the members of the group lie down in a star formation. People's heads should be in the center, which represents the brightness of the star; they should be close together but not touching. People's bodies should project out from the center like the rays of the star, their legs slightly apart (figure 1, page 128). If you are working alone, your body orientation does not matter, but your legs should be slightly apart.

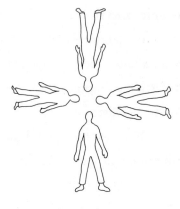

FIGURE 1

Be aware of two areas of your body. The first is your Will area, which is one to one-and-a-half inches below your belly button. Focus your attention and place your quartz crystal on your Will area. Your power is reclaimed and manifested through your Will. The second area to be aware of is Silent Knowledge. It is above the center of the top of your head, your crown chakra. Silent Knowledge is your knowledge of everything that exists in the Dream of the Planet and in life. Silent Knowledge is inside you. In order to open the door to Silent Knowledge, you have to open the door to the memories of your life, including your wounds.

Take some deep breaths and surrender to Mother Earth, keeping your awareness focused on your Will area. Visualize the energy of Silent Knowledge moving down from the center of your head, traveling along your throat, passing through your lungs, and connecting to your Will. As Silent Knowledge connects to your Will, they become one (figure 2). Visualize them reaching out to the sun through a beautiful ray of light that stretches from your Will area.

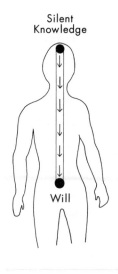

FIGURE 2

At this first level of Stalking, focus on what happened during your day. If you are Stalking in the evening, recall everything that happened that day up until the time you started Stalking. If you are Stalking in the morning, focus on everything that occurred the previous day. Start with the first moment you opened your eyes. What were your first thoughts? What were the first words out of your mouth? Then where did you go and what did you do? What were your thoughts about other people, your workplace, and the other environments you were in? As you review the whole day, and visualize each image, use the Stalking technique. Reclaim the thoughts, agreements, and energy you gave to other people with your in-breath, filtering them through your body into Mother Earth. With your out-breath, use your love to give back anything that was given to you, such as agreements and harsh language.

3. Reflection. Once you have completed Stalking, sit up. Reflect on your experience. If you are Stalking alone, write in a journal or speak into a tape recorder. Include the date and what you Stalked that day. Describe what came up for you, how you cleaned it, and what you are now feeling. If you are working with a group, share your experiences with the other people. The role of the group members is only to listen, not to offer advice, judgments, or any other "help." They are there to support you by listening to your experiences, nothing else. This is not a therapy session. After sharing with the group, write your experiences in a journal, or speak into a tape recorder. Journals are important tools for healing and for documenting your inner journey.

4. Closing Meditation for Healing. After you complete the reflection phase, lie down again and close your eyes. Take a few deep breaths and relax. Visualize a huge ray of light extending from the sun into your heart. See the ray of light touch all the wounded areas that you cleaned in Stalking. As the remaining energy from the wounds is released, these areas will expand with the beautiful, healing ray of light from the sun. Feel the light warming your heart and traveling through your whole body. Feel the rhythm of your breathing. Now visualize the small version of you that entered your heart during the opening meditation. Then focus on all the different images of you that you Stalked today. One by one, visualize each image entering your body, walking through your mouth, continuing down your throat, and finally passing through the door into your heart. See the small version of you in your heart embrace each image as it walks in, welcoming it into your temple. After the last image enters your heart, see all of them merge into one being, who is the person you are now. With each breath visualize gentleness, patience, and self-forgiveness. Continue breathing deeply. Now visualize your breath going out to the people you focused on in your Stalking session. Your breath is pure love. Then send this love to your family, to other people you love, to your home, and to the world. Always know that the ray of light from the sun is inside you every moment. You are never separate from it. When you have finished sending love with your breath, you can sit up. The Stalking session is complete.

For the next several weeks continue focusing, during Stalking, on your experiences throughout the day, or since your last Stalking session. This will help you get the rhythm of Stalking. You will also start to see agreements at work in your daily life. After several weeks, expand your Stalking sessions to include the most recent relationship in your life. Visualize yourself in that relationship. How do you see yourself? Do you see yourself with respect? How do the two of you treat each other? Are you sincere? Do you speak your truth and communicate clearly? Look at the wounds you have in that relationship; see the patterns and find the agreements given to you. Once you have completed Stalking this most recent relationship, go backward in time and Stalk each relationship in your life, back to the point that you first started dating. This work will probably take you three to five months, depending both upon your personal experiences, which are somewhat related to your age, and upon how frequently you Stalk.

LEVEL 2 STALKING: ALIGNMENT OF ENERGY
Items needed:
quartz crystal that fits in the palm of your hand
pillow for your head
rug or blanket to lie on
journal or tape recorder

1. Heart Meditation. The Heart Meditation opens your heart in preparation for Stalking.

Lie on your back on the floor inside your house, or outside on the ground. Place your palms flat, facing down. For comfort, you can use a pillow for your head and lie on a blanket or rug. Close your eyes. Take some deep breaths and focus on relaxing yourself. Feel your body lying on the ground and totally surrender yourself to Mother Earth. Let go of any physical tension you are holding, and any thoughts in your mind. Focus on the rhythm of your breath.

After a few moments, visualize a small version of yourself at this moment in your life. See this small version of you entering your mouth and then walking through your mouth and down your throat toward your heart. As you get near your heart, visualize a door. Since you are creating this door, it can appear any way you want. It can be made of the most beautiful gold, or be intricately carved out of wood, or just be very simple. Whatever works for you. Then open the door and enter your heart. Look inside your heart with honest eyes. What do you see? Who are the people you love that you carry inside your heart? This is the time to let them go free. The people you love do not belong to you; love is not controlling. This moment is about releasing the images you have created of these people out of love. Let their spirits fly. To do so, first thank them for being there in your heart. Then as you breathe out, release them one at a time. Continue breathing out and releasing them until you feel complete. When you are done, visualize a beautiful ray of light from the sun inside your heart. This ray of light is pure love, and it will nourish and stay with you always. After a few moments, open your eyes.

The intent of this meditation is to clean your heart, the purest temple that ever existed, and to fill it with pure love. The little version of you now lives in your heart. Because of this, you will love yourself more and more unconditionally each time you complete this meditation. You will also respect yourself as you would the highest queen, king, guru, or other image of purity. That image of purity is you.

2. Stalking. As in the first level of Stalking, continue to lie down on the floor of your house or the ground outside with your palms flat. You can also continue to use a pillow for your head and a blanket to lie on. If you are working with a group, have the members lie in two rows. The first row of people should lie side-by-side, with their shoulders close but not touching. The second row of people should lie the same way, but with their bodies extended in the opposite direction and their heads about one inch from the heads of the people in the first row. Each person's head should be aligned with one other person's head, so that

people work in pairs. Therefore,
it is best to have an even number
of people (figure 3). Working
alone is also fine, in which case
your body orientation does not
matter. Everyone's legs should
be slightly apart.

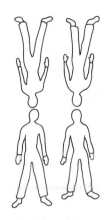

As in the first level of Stalking, place your quartz crystal
over your Will area. Then vi-

FIGURE 3

sualize the energy of Silent Knowledge descending from
your crown chakra and connecting to your Will. The two
energies become one, and from your Will area a brilliant
ray of light projects out to the sun.

At this second level, you are Stalking the agreements
given to you by your mother and father. If your parents
are alive, focus on your most recent experiences with
them. If one or both of your parents are deceased, call up
from memory your most recent interactions. Begin with
your most recent memories and move backward in time
as far as you can recall. Look at the situations. See the
things that upset you and caused you to react. Visualize
how you communicated. Reclaim the energy you gave
to your parents using your in-breath. Then, using your
out-breath, send love to your parents and return to them

anything that was given to you. Call up one scene or image at a time, and focus on it until you feel complete. Go as far back in time as you can recall.

3. Reflection. Once you have completed Stalking, sit up. Reflect on your experiences. Write or tape-record what you saw, speaking your truth to yourself. If you are working with a group, share your experiences with the other people, again speaking your truth. This is an opportunity for members of the group to refine their level of listening. After sharing with the group, write or record what you saw for yourself.

4. Closing Meditation for Healing. After you complete the reflection phase, lie down again and close your eyes. Take a few deep breaths and relax. Visualize a huge ray of light extending from the sun into your heart. See the ray of light touch all the wounded areas that you cleaned in Stalking. As the remaining energy from the wounds is released, these areas will expand with the beautiful, healing ray of light from the sun. Feel the light warming your heart and traveling through your whole body. Feel the rhythm of your breathing. Now visualize the small version of you that entered your heart during the opening meditation. Then focus on the different images of you that you Stalked today. Visualize each image entering your body, walking through your mouth, continuing down your throat, and finally passing through the door into your heart. See the small version of you in your heart embrace each image as it walks in, welcoming it into your temple. After the last image enters your heart, see all of them merge into one being, who is the person you are now. With each breath visualize gentleness, patience, and self-forgiveness. Continue breathing deeply. Now visualize your breath going out to your parents. Your breath is pure love. Then send this love to your whole family, to other people you love, to your home, and to the world. Always know that the ray of light from the sun is inside you every moment. You are never separate from it. When you have finished sending love with your breath, you can sit up. The Stalking session is complete.

For the next several months continue focusing, during Stalking, on your relationship with your parents. Start with your current age and then go backward in time. Stalk your experiences with your parents at each age for approximately a week. Take your memories back as far as you can, until you were very little. The length of time necessary to complete this second level of Stalking will depend upon your age and how frequently you

Stalk. If you are thirty years old, it will probably take you about six months to complete this level if your memories go back to age six. If you Stalk daily, it may take less than a week to cover each age. Also, some ages will have fewer memories for you than other ages.

LEVEL 3 STALKING: THE DIRECTIONS

Items needed:

pillow for your head and to sit on

rug or blanket to lie on

journal or tape recorder

1. Heart Meditation. The Heart Meditation opens your heart in preparation for Stalking.

Lie on your back on the floor inside your house, or outside on the ground. Place your palms flat, facing down. For comfort, you can use a pillow for your head and lie on a blanket or rug. Close your eyes. Take some deep breaths and focus on relaxing yourself. Feel your body lying on the ground and totally surrender yourself to Mother Earth. Let go of any physical tension you are holding, and any thoughts in your mind. Focus on the rhythm of your breath.

After a few moments, visualize a small version of yourself at this moment in your life. See this small version of you entering your mouth and then walking through your mouth and down your throat toward your heart. As you get near your heart, visualize a door. Since you are creating this door, it can appear any way you want. It can be made of the most beautiful gold, or be intricately carved out of wood, or just be very simple. Whatever works for you. Then open the door and enter your heart. Look inside your heart with honest eyes. What do you see? Who are the people you love that you carry inside your heart? This is the time to let them go free. The people you love do not belong to you; love is not controlling. This moment is about releasing the images you have created of these people out of love. Let their spirits fly. To do so, first thank them for being there in your heart. Then, as you breathe out, release them one at a time. Continue breathing out and releasing them until you feel complete. When you are done, visualize a beautiful ray of light from the sun inside your heart. This ray of light is pure love, and it will nourish and stay with you always. After a few moments, open your eyes.

The intent of this meditation is to clean your heart, the purest temple that ever existed, and to fill it with pure love. The little version of you now lives in your heart. Because of this, you will love yourself more and more unconditionally each time you complete this meditation. You will also respect yourself as you would the highest queen, king, guru, or other image of purity. That image of purity is you.

2. Stalking. Once you complete the Heart Meditation, sit up. Do this third level of Stalking in a sitting position. Bend your knees, keep your legs slightly apart, and place your feet flat on the floor. Rest your arms on top of your knees. You can do this either inside your house or outside.

FIGURES 4 AND 5

If you are Stalking with other people, work in a group of four. Sit in a circle facing outward, with your shoulders touching. Each of you faces a different direction, north, south, east, or west (figure 4, side view; figure 5, top view).

Visualize the energy of Silent Knowledge descending through your body and joining with your Will. At this third level of Stalking, however, Silent Knowledge and your Will extend from your body in two different directions. See the energy of Silent Knowledge projecting out to the sun in a beautiful ray of light. See your Will projecting out to the direction you face in a beautiful ray of light. They are still one, however. This visualization results in powerful connections between the direction you face, the sun, and your whole self.

At this third level, you are Stalking your agreements with your relatives and friends. If you have brothers, sisters, stepbrothers, or stepsisters, this is the time to Stalk your relationships with them. Take some deep breaths. With your in-breath, reclaim the energy you have given out to these relatives. Send it to Mother Earth. Since you are sitting up rather than lying down, the energy moves down through your spine into Mother Earth. With your out-breath return the energy to those who gave you any agreements.

3. Reflection. Once you have completed Stalking, reflect on your experiences. Write or tape-record what you saw, speaking your truth to yourself. If you are working with a group, share your experiences with the other people, again speaking your truth. After sharing with the group, write or record your experiences for yourself.

4. Closing Meditation for Healing. After you complete the reflection phase, lie down and close your eyes. Take a few deep breaths and relax. Visualize a huge ray of light extending from the sun into your heart. See the ray of light touch all the wounded areas that you cleaned in Stalking. As the remaining energy from the wounds is released, these areas will expand with the beautiful, healing ray of light from the sun. Feel the light warming your heart and traveling through your whole body. Feel the rhythm of your breathing. Now visualize the small version of you that entered your heart during the opening meditation. Then focus on the different images of you that you Stalked today. Visualize each image entering your body, walking through your mouth, continuing down your throat, and finally passing through the door into your heart. See the small version of you in your heart embrace each image as it walks in, welcoming it into your temple. After the last image enters your heart, see all of them merge into one being, who is the person you are now. With each breath visualize gentleness, patience, and self-forgiveness. Continue breathing deeply. Now visualize your breath going out to the relatives you focused on in your Stalking session. Your breath is pure love. Then send this love to your whole family, to other people you love, to your home, and to the world. Always know that the ray of light from the sun is inside you every moment. You are never separate from it. When you have finished sending love with your breath, you can sit up. The Stalking session is complete.

Completing this third level of Stalking will take about

six months. During this time, Stalk your interactions with other relatives—your uncles, aunts, cousins, and so on—and with your friends. Start with more recent interactions and go backward in time. For one-and-a-half months, face the first direction you chose. After this time, rotate to face a new direction for the next one-and-a-half months. Continue rotating directions every one-and-a-half months until you have faced all four directions.

LEVEL 4 STALKING: SHATTERING IMAGES

Items needed:

journal or tape recorder

pillow for your head

rug or blanket to lie on

1. Heart Meditation. The Heart Meditation opens your heart in preparation for Stalking.

Lie on your back on the floor inside your house, or outside on the ground. Place your palms flat, facing down. For comfort, you can use a pillow for your head and lie on a blanket or rug. Close your eyes. Take some deep breaths and focus on relaxing yourself. Feel your body lying on the ground and totally surrender yourself to Mother Earth. Let go of any physical tension you are holding, and any thoughts in your mind. Focus on the rhythm of your breath.

After a few moments, visualize a small version of yourself at this moment in your life. See this small version of you entering your mouth and then walking through your mouth and down your throat toward your heart. As you get near your heart, visualize a door. Since you are creating this door, it can appear any way you want. It can be made of the most beautiful gold, or be intricately carved out of wood, or just be very simple. Whatever works for you. Then open the door and enter your heart. Look inside your heart with honest eyes. What do you see? Who are the people you love that you carry inside your heart? This is the time to let them go free. The people you love do not belong to you; love is not controlling. This moment is about releasing the images you have created of these people out of love. Let their spirits fly. To do so, first thank them for being there in your heart. Then, as you breathe out, release them one at a time. Continue breathing out and releasing them until you feel complete. When you are done, visualize a beautiful ray of light from the sun inside your heart. This ray of light is pure love, and it will nourish and stay with you always. After a few moments, open your eyes.

The intent of this meditation is to clean your heart, the purest temple that ever existed, and to fill it with pure love. The little version of you now lives in your heart. Because of this, you will love yourself more and more unconditionally each time you complete this meditation. You will also respect yourself as you would the highest queen, king, guru, or other image of purity. That image of purity is you.

2. Stalking. Stalking is very different at this fourth level because it involves the shattering of images. At this stage, you break any huge agreements, such as those associated with abusive memories. You let them go. Throughout Stalking, you remain standing up. You begin Stalking with the Jaguar Movement for about five minutes and then move on to Shattering Images.

The Jaguar Movement. The jaguar is an animal that is always alert and ready for action. Begin the Jaguar Movement by standing alertly, your knees bent a little and your weight slightly forward, as if you are about to start running. Let your arms hang loosely at your side. Then bend your arms at the elbow; your right forearm is now out in front of your body. Move this arm to the level of your head, place your palm down,

FIGURE 6

with your fingers slightly cupped or relaxed. Your left forearm, at your side and bent at the elbow, is out in front of your body at your hip level. Place the hand palm up, with your fingers slightly cupped or relaxed. Breathe deeply and then shift your weight from one leg to the other, moving up and down very slowly; you are weaving back and forth (figure 6, page 145).

Move your arms up and down in rhythm with your legs. Bring your right, elevated arm down, and bring your left arm up. As your right arm reaches hip level, flip your right hand to a palm-up position. As your left arm reaches the level of your head, flip your left hand to a palm-down position. Then bring your right arm back up to its starting position and your left arm back down to its starting position. Flip your right and left hands at the same time. As your legs weave back and forth, your arms move up and down and your palms flip position simultaneously at the

FIGURE 7

top and bottom of the movement. The overall movement is like that of a jaguar running. The intent of this movement is to spin an energy weaving of Mother Earth and

the sun. This weaving helps you break the agreements
(figure 7, page 146).

Do the Jaguar Movement for at least five minutes and
then stop. Come to a stable, balanced position with your
arms at your sides. Then raise your arms in front of you
to the middle of your body. Clap your hands forcibly together and then rub them quickly until they feel like they
are on fire.

Visualize Silent Knowledge and your Will connect-
ing once again in your Will area. For this fourth level,
see the energies going straight up your spine and out your
crown chakra.

Shattering Images. Visualize
an image and its accompanying
agreement that you wish to give
back to someone. See the image
breaking away from you and moving off into the universe. Then see
it shatter like a window, breaking
into a million pieces. Visualize
those pieces turning into energy,
which moves away from you and
returns with intent to the person who gave you the agreement. As you visualize the energy moving away from you,
breathe out forcibly. Extend your right arm and rotate it

FIGURE 8

counterclockwise one-and-a-half times. Stop the rotation with your arm over the center of your head. Then bring your arm down the center of your body, as if it were a sword. Move it past your eyes, throat, lungs, stomach, and first chakra area. This movement cuts any energy cords that connect you to the agreement (figure 8, page 147).

Next, pull both your arms back with your palms extended outward. Then forcibly push your arms and hands forward as if you are pushing something away from your body. Your intention is to separate the energy cords from you and push them away (figure 9).

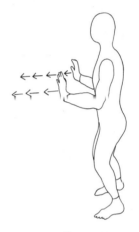

FIGURE 9

Continue to shatter images until you feel complete. Then do the Jaguar Movement again. Afterward, clap and rub your hands together until they are hot with energy. Then gently move your hands over your body, cleaning each area. Clean your eyes so you may see with clearer vision. Clean your ears so you may hear truth. Clean your throat so you may speak your truth every moment, and so you may cry, laugh, and sing when you want to. Clean the back of your neck and the top of your head to release energy. Touch your whole body to cleanse it. At the same time, have the greatest gratitude for the service your body performs for you every moment. Your body is your servant, so treat it and yourself with the greatest love and respect.

3. Closing Meditation for Healing. After Stalking, remain standing in the Jaguar position. Close your eyes and visualize a being that you have looked up to, such as a saint, a guru, Jesus, or Allah. See that being in your heart and visualize yourself becoming one with him or her, the energy traveling through each part of your body, touching any area that is ill, that has experienced any abuse, or that holds any agreements. After focusing on each part of your body, remain in silence and stillness for a short while. Then visualize your breath going out to the people you focused on in your Stalking. Your breath is pure love. Send this love to your family, to other people you love, to your home, and to the world. Always know that the ray of light from the sun is inside you every moment. You are never separate from it. When you have finished sending love with your breath, the Stalking session is complete.

4. Reflection. Once you have completed Stalking and the Closing Meditation for Healing, reflect on your experiences. Write or tape-record your experiences, speaking your truth to yourself. If you are working with a group, share your experiences with the other people, again speaking your truth. Be a focused listener. After sharing with the group, write or record your experiences for yourself.

Focus on this fourth level of Stalking for three to four months. At this stage, you have passed the level of the Jaguar Knight and are working at the Eagle Knight level. The jaguar will always be inside you, but you are now taking flight and becoming the eagle. The eagle soars and has an expanded perception. It sees the broad view and the focused view at the same moment. The work at this level is about finding freedom and expanding your perception. At this level of Stalking, you have reclaimed a lot of energy and are holding much more personal power. You are seeing your life change. Your awareness in the moment has grown, you are enjoying life more, you are making true choices, and you are being truthful with yourself.

As you progress, notice that your perception and awareness become very fine-tuned. You see life in such a new way, it is as if you never saw it before. More and more you choose to create an environment that makes you content. The people you choose to associate with share your level of vision. They do not go against you, and you do not go against them. You feel a great appreciation for life, and view everything as the beautiful warrior you are. You truly love and respect yourself.

LEVEL 5 STALKING: ONENESS

Items needed:

a sturdy chair

1. Stalking. This is the last level of Stalking. It is the mastery level of the Eagle Knight warrior. It is the level of oneness. At this stage, you develop the awareness that everything is yourself because everything comes from your own senses and emotions. You do not need to give anything back during Stalking because everything that you visualize is yourself.

At this level of Stalking, there is no Heart Meditation. Sit on a sturdy chair, with your feet flat on the floor and your palms flat on your lap. Your legs should be slightly apart. Close your eyes and remain still. Breathe normally.

Focus on your Divine Will, which is in your third eye, in the center of your forehead. Send a beautiful ray of light out from the Divine Will to the sun. Visualize yourself as the sun, with rays of light extending from you in all directions. Now visualize the image of anything you are still reacting to or feeling judgment about. See that image as yourself. It is not separate from you. It is you. Take the image inside yourself as the sun, and transform it into light. Breathe it in as a ray of sunlight inside yourself. Do not send it out to anybody. It is transformed inside you. See the image as everything that exists: the trees, the flowers, the weeds. And since everything is yourself, nothing can ever cause you to react again.

The intent of this level of Stalking is to see yourself as the ray of light that is pure love. Pure love is everything. You are everything. Everything is you.

After you feel complete, take a few moments to send your love to the whole Dream of the Planet with each out-breath. Especially send your love to those who are being raped or killed, and to those who are suffering. Visualize them knowing and feeling the ray of love around them.

2. Reflection. If you are working alone, write or record your experiences. If you are working in a group, share with the other people first.

There is no set time frame for completing this fifth level of Stalking. Continue as long as you feel that it is important for your growth or until you feel there is no separation between you and everything else that exists.

In Summary: Things to Keep in Mind for All Levels of Stalking

Remember to have fun as you work through each level of Stalking, whether you are alone or in a group. Always be truthful with yourself and others, be impeccable, and surrender every moment. Don't be afraid to feel what you feel and be honest about it. You can't run away from your anger, your sadness, or your Judge. They may hide for a while, and continue to build inside you. Then all of a sudden something will trigger them, and the emotions or judgments will be expressed with much greater intensity. So when you are Stalking, it is all right to cry and release emotions. But always be in the moment. Focus on your breathing and just surrender. Be aware of what you are feeling, but don't let the emotions consume you. Feel them and let them go. Love the anger, the Judge, and the Victim. Embrace the jealousy. You are loving, embracing, and acknowledging the wounded child within you. Acknowledgment is healing. It is the acknowledgment and the embrace that create forgiveness and love for yourself.

12

THE SPIRAL

The Final Battle

AS YOU MOVE THROUGH THE DIFFERENT LEVELS OF
Stalking, you may find that you continue to experience a
particular agreement. An emotion or pattern based on
that agreement keeps coming up for you. You have looked
at that agreement many times, cleaning and releasing it.
Then all of a sudden it is there again, and this time the
feeling based on the agreement is even more magnified,
even more intense. It feels like the emotion is expanding. What is really happening is that your own ray of
light, which is the energy you have gathered around you
from Stalking, is expanding. You have reclaimed a lot of

your energy, and in doing so your ray of light and love and respect has grown tremendously. Therefore, when you face the emotion of the agreement again, you have a larger ray of light shining on it, so it looks and feels more intense. This is the spiral.

Visualize yourself traveling along a road that begins at the bottom of a mountain. As you continue on the road, you circle the mountain as you climb upward, eventually reaching the top of the mountain. Once you reach the peak, you can see that the road forms a spiral. You are inside this spiral, which forms a peak at your head and gets wider as it extends to your feet.

The peak of the spiral is the center of your spiritual being. This is where the memory of your life is contained. Your rays of light originate at this peak and then project down to the bottom of the spiral. In those rays of light are the tunnels of agreements. When you begin Stalking, you start at the bottom of the spiral. As you continue Stalking, you climb the spiral and look at the agreements along the way. At one point you hit a certain agreement, and then as you climb higher on the spiral, you circle around and hit the same agreement again, farther up its tunnel. The second time you hit the agreement you are facing it in a different vibration of light because you are higher on the spiral. As you

Stalk and you climb, you are cleaning the tunnel of that agreement, so you face it a number of times before you reach the top.

The key is not to get discouraged as you continue Stalking. You may reach an agreement that you have already Stalked numerous times before. But there it is again. Remember, what this means is that you have reached a new level on the spiral and are now cleaning that agreement with a different ray of light. The emotion may be more intense because you have reclaimed your energy as you have Stalked and you are now looking at the agreement with a bigger energy field.

When the emotion comes up, no matter how strong, it is important to stay in the moment and look at the agreement. The magnified energy that you have gathered during Stalking is being given to that emotion, which is the Parasite. So the emotion is even more intense. Know that it is okay to feel what you are feeling. But stay in the moment of each breath. Don't run away from the feeling or think that it is wrong to have it. Just love it. When you love the feeling, you are loving yourself.

Your intent as a warrior is to go up the spiral and clean the multiple agreements that surround it. Eventually, you reach the center point of all agreements. When you reach this center point of the spiral, you face the final battle with the emotion of the agreements, or the Parasite. You are then facing the dragon, your own personal emotional beast. When you are in such a state of emotion, you may feel like you have become a beast or a monster. That feeling is extreme.

However, by this time your personal awareness has grown enough that you are able to stay in the moment and not allow the Parasite to take all your attention. This moment may feel very strange to you. You may feel a way that you have never felt before. You are alone with yourself, facing yourself. You are at peace, and yet you are facing your belief system, who you thought you were, and who everybody else thought you were based on the agreements you were told. But now the agreement tunnels are all clean, and your ray of light is huge at the top of the peak. The true you is facing the you that was wounded and unhappy, in a state of hell on earth.

Birth of the Angel

The final battle is a time to be still with yourself: to chant, meditate, stay in the moment, stay with your breath, love your breath and yourself, breathe in love, and breathe out love. Your process may last a week, more or less. Stay focused in the moment and treat yourself well. Take a trip. Sit in a hot tub. Go see a movie. Be gentle with yourself. Eventually all the little beings inside you that you visualize in the Heart Meditation merge into one—the big universe that is you. When you surrender to the true you, the part of you that is the pure angel manifests. You become one with yourself and with everything. You have a new birth, and you see life with new eyes. You become the most radiant being that exists, you feel at peace, and you truly live life for the first time. This is freedom.

For information about future lectures, workshops, and power journeys, visit doña Bernadette Vigil's Web site at www.BernadetteVigil.com. You can join her e-mailing list by sending a message to mailinglist@BernadetteVigil.com.